Start Your Own

AUTOMOBILE DETAILING BUSINESS

Additional titles in *Entrepreneur's **Startup Series***

Start Your Own

start up

Start Your Own

2ND EDITION

AUTOMOBILE DETAILING BUSINESS

Your Step-by-Step
Guide to Success

Entrepreneur Press and Rich Mintzer

Jere L. Calmes, Publisher
Cover Design: Beth Hansen-Winter
Composition and Production: MillerWorks

This publication is designed to provide accurate and authoritative information
in regard to the subject matter covered. It is sold with the understanding that the
publisher is not engaged in rendering legal, accounting or other professional services.
If legal advice or other expert assistance is required, the services of a
competent professional person should be sought.

Library of Congress Cataloging-in-Publication Data Available

Mintzer, Richard.
    Start your own automobile detailing business/By Entrepreneur Press and Rich
Mintzer. — 2nd. ed.
        p. cm. — (Start your own series)
    Rev. ed. of: Start your own automobile detailing business/Entrepreneur Press
and Eileen Figure Sandlin, 2005.
    Includes index.
    ISBN 978-1-59918-176-9 (alk. paper)
    1. Automobile detailing. 2. New business enterprises—Management. 3. Small
business. I. Mintzer, Richard. II. Entrepreneur Press.

TL152.15.S26 2008
629.28'7—dc22   2008004712

Printed in Canada

10 09 08   10 9 8 7 6 5 4 3 2 1

Contents

Chapter 9

Owner's Manual:
Your Guide to Professional Development 109

Chapter 10

Driving the Competition 115

Chapter 11

Internet Marketing and Research 131

Chapter 12

Tooting Your Own Horn. 139

Preface

It's a dirty job, but somebody's got to do it... and now that you've made the decision to be a professional automobile detailer, you could be the one who turns water into dollar signs.

Automobile detailing has been a hot industry for enterprising entrepreneurs for more than a decade. Some experts believe the trend toward detailing as a profession was spawned by the sharp spike in new-car sticker prices that began in the '80s, which induced thrifty Americans to hold onto their vehicles way past their expiration date. Others think the industry was spawned by the entrepreneurial spirit that gripped

America throughout the '90s, persuading frazzled 9-to-5ers to escape from high-stress jobs and plunge into self-employment ventures that didn't force them to sacrifice their quality of life. The fact that the average car price nearly doubled between 2002 and 2005, (before dropping off slightly by 2007), has also given rise to a profession that may allow a car owner to keep his or her older vehicle looking and running well a few years longer. Still others feel detailing has evolved into a popular startup business simply because the initial costs are fairly low and the potential for profit is as high as the detailer's ambition.

Ambition is just one of the traits a new automotive detailer needs for success. Meticulous attention to detail, patience, and a gift of gab also come in handy. A genuine love of anything with horses under the hood and four on the floor doesn't hurt, either.

Since running your own business means that you will be responsible for everything from obtaining financing to paying the bills, it also helps to have at least a basic aptitude for numbers and some business basics. Previous high school or college coursework in disciplines like accounting and business management can be very beneficial. But don't be concerned if your education has been a little light on financial know-how. Between the business professionals who can help keep your books and do your taxes and your own motivation, you can be successful in this field.

In this book, you'll find all the practical advice you'll need to build an automotive detailing business from the chassis up. That includes information you'll need to handle the myriad details that go into starting and operating a small business—from analyzing your market, writing a business plan, and establishing an internet presence to finding the financing and handling all the other day-to-day duties necessary to keep your business running like a well-oiled machine. There are worksheets to help you calculate costs, keep expenditures under control, and stay organized. There also are names and mailing addresses (both snail and cyber) of numerous industry organizations, suppliers, and government agencies that can provide answers and ideas.

But perhaps most important, there are words of wisdom throughout this book from auto detailers and industry experts who have unique insight into the behind-the-scenes process of running a professional detailing business.

Incidentally, you won't find instructions in these pages for buffing paint to a mirror finish or removing swirls. Frankly, that instruction is best left to the pros who teach detailing techniques, including the companies that make the detailing chemicals you'll be using. You'll find information about instructional opportunities in Chapter 9 and in the Appendix.

Because people come into this industry with different resources and expectations, we've covered techniques for starting a business both on a shoestring and on a big budget supercharged with cash. So now, let's shift into gear. This is gonna be the ride of your life!

Start Your
Engines

When it comes to an industry with wide-open opportunities for enterprising small-business owners, auto detailing ranks right up there with the best of them.

And small wonder. Americans' passion for cars, coupled with busy, fast-paced lifestyles that leave them with little time to take care of those vehicles properly, has created an environment rife with potential for today's aspiring detailer. Just consider this: A recent survey by carlove.org indicated that 84 percent of American car owners love or like their cars, but only 15 percent of those take excellent care of the object of their affection. Does that mean the other 69 percent could be your customers? You bet!

So, What Is Auto Detailing?

A basic and fundamentally broad definition of auto detailing might be: To clean, polish, and enhance the overall appearance of an automobile by taking special care of the car's individual details. Of course, this does not take into account the level, or quality, of service necessary to separate detailing from simply cleaning. This has spawned a great debate between long-time devoted detailers and the more recent "quickie" detailing offered at car washes and other locales. Essentially, the term "detailing" has become heavily marketed to a public that is not familiar with the difference between a good interior and exterior cleaning and a meticulous detailing job. However, as detailing emerges and more businesses (like yours) open up, the public will begin to see the different levels possible and make their own assessment of what they consider to be a real (quality) detailing job.

You can also define detailing in conjunction with the portion of the car being detailed. For example, exterior detailing can include claying, polishing, and waxing, while interior detailing involves the cleaning of the interior of a vehicle using vacuums, liquid cleaners, and brushes. Engine detailing involves cleaning the engine bay area of dirt and grease by using degreasers and all-purpose cleaners.

It's also worth mentioning that detailing can be defined differently by those who are seeking such service. For example, to someone whose vehicle will be in upcoming car shows, detailing means "show ready," while someone looking to sell a car might define detailing as a process that increases the value of the vehicle with a well-maintained finish.

The Big Picture

Despite the detailing industry's enormous earning potential and small-business opportunities, there is surprisingly little information available about it in terms of statistics and trends. The industry doesn't have its own professional association (the closest thing is the International Carwash Association, which has a detailing component). What little statistical information is available on the numbers of detailers, wages,

Bright Idea

A lot of people don't know the difference between detailing (restoring) and customizing (adding nifty extras like fancy wheels). Be sure to explain exactly what you do in your promotional materials and Yellow Pages ad.

and other pertinent information is several years old. Even the federal government doesn't pay much attention to the profession (except for the IRS, that is). Detailers aren't singled out in the Bureau of Labor Statistics' Occupational Outlook Handbook (published by the U.S. Department of Labor); rather, they're included in the "Equipment Cleaners, Helpers, and Laborers" category (which no doubt includes those who clean everything from industrial manufacturing machinery to dry cleaning equipment).

Stat Fact

According to the latest statistics, as researched by RL "Bud" Abraham, founder and president of Detail Plus Car Appearance Systems. There are 14,000 independent detailer businesses listed in the United States Yellow Pages, up from 4,000 in 1980.

Likewise, the Bureau of the Census has a similar "Cleaners of Vehicles and Equipment" category, which presumably includes carwash employees. But the Census Bureau offers no other information about these employees the way it does for hair stylists, longshoremen, and other professionals.

"There's not a lot of official recognition for this profession and no statistics," confirms auto reconditioning expert Prentice St. Clair, owner of Detail in Progress in San Diego. "That's probably because it's such an easy business to get into that three-quarters of the businesses are 'under the radar.'"

Historical Perspective

Although detailing came into its own as an industry fairly recently, the profession actually dates back to the days of the horse-drawn carriage, which were lovingly hand polished and spit-shined. But it really gathered steam with the advent of vehicles that had the horses under rather than in front. One of the pioneers in what would become the detailing product industry was furniture polish maker Frank Meguiar, Jr., who, in 1901, mixed bottles of wood polish one at a time using an eggbeater. He soon realized that his product also could be used on those early automobiles, which were made of wood and coated with the same finishes used on furniture, and a new industry was born.

Until the 1940s, owners of elite motorcars were the most frequent consumers of detailing services. Then, after World War II, car dealership owners realized that reconditioning previously owned cars would increase their value and thereby increase the dealers' profit margins. As a result, many dealerships added full-service detailing departments, which soon were prepping new cars for delivery. But the recessions of 1980 and 1982 forced many dealers to reduce or lay off their detailing staff, which opened the door to new opportunities for independent detailers.

Not coincidentally, the consumer detailing market started to heat up around the same time. As cars became more expensive, consumers started keeping their vehicles for longer periods of time. In 1969, for example, when the average price of a new car was $3,708, consumers kept their cars an average of just over three years. By 2001, there were 216 million vehicles in use (40 percent of which were trucks), and the average price of a new car had increased to $14,449. Likewise, the length of time consumers kept their cars increased to an average of nine years. Increasing at an unparalleled rate, the average sticker price for a new car or light truck more than doubled, jumping to $30,481 by December of 2003, according to an analysis by auto price tracker Edmunds.com. As of late 2007, the average new car sticker price had dipped slightly to roughly $28,000. According to Edmonds.com, there are also now more than 40 million used cars purchased each year (for an average of roughly $14,000) and an estimated 17 million new cars purchased annually. Today, people are keeping cars nearly 10 years, making it more important than ever to maintain them, and making detailing more prevalent.

Another factor also influenced Americans' predilection to keep their cars longer: The federal government erased the tax deduction for auto loan and credit card interest in the '80s. Suddenly, a new car loan was an even greater liability than before, and people started looking at their trusty old cars with infinitely more fondness. All this thriftiness represents a great opportunity for a new detailer. Many owners of older vehicles want to keep their rides in top condition, particularly those vehicles that have weathered a couple of presidential administrations. But keep in mind that people who wash their cars at home in the driveway are not likely to be your customers. The 2002 International Carwash Association Study of Consumer Car Washing Attitudes and Habits indicated that nearly 86 percent of home washers who responded to the survey had not had their car detailed in the previous year. So your challenge will be to find the consumers who take pride in their vehicles but don't have the time or inclination to keep them looking showroom-ready.

Notes from the Dean

You'll probably notice quotes and comments from R.L. "Bud" Abraham throughout the book; Bud has spent nearly 40 years in the business, and is still going strong as the founder and president of Detail Plus Car Appearance Systems. Over the past four decades he had been in the auto detailing industry as an operator, distributor, manufacturer, and consultant. Bud has personally designed and built car care centers including detailing and car wash businesses all over the world, and has owned and personally operated detail centers and automatic carwash facilities. A regular speaker at industry events, he is known as the "Dean of Detailing" by many of the top pros in the field.

According to Bud, the business has grown significantly since the late 1970's when detailing meant "restorative" detailing. "There was a lot more do-it-yourself work done thirty years ago. People bought Simonize and wax products and took care of cleaning their cars themselves. Today, with both husbands and wives working, car care is something that people prefer to pay for. Not many people do this for themselves any longer," explains Abraham, of a field that has expanded from restorative to appearance and maintenance generated.

While the size of the industry has increased, and there is greater potential for earnings, in some ways the industry hasn't changed very much, acknowledges Abraham. "You still have a lot of guys using shop vacs, portable steam cleaners, and chemicals in the plastic bottles. There is a lot of new technology, but many detailers like to stick to how they've been doing things for years," says Abraham, adding that for some businesses that can work out fine, while others have benefited from new technology.

Abraham also points out that the detailing industry does not have a "standard in the industry" in the way that Jiffy Lube or Starbucks have set the standard and raised the bar their industries. "The industry has never had a major company take the lead. It's still very much a cottage industry," adds Abraham, which is a plus for newcomers in the business who don't have to aspire to some level that is potentially out of their reach. However, it makes it difficult for consumers to know what a high-quality detailing facility should look like or have a means of comparison as they would if they walked into a coffee house, which they could compare to Starbucks.

For those who are ready to embrace the latest in technology, Abraham's Detail Plus Car Appearance Systems offers the latest in technology for speeding up the process and making the job that much easier. For example, rather than manually handling numerous bottles of chemicals and mixing each one with water, Detail Plus sells a chemical dispensing system that is similar to those used by car washes whereby similar chemicals are automatically diluted and automatically dispensed by pumps. "We run lines for carpet shampoo, glass cleaner, all purpose cleaner and so on, so that the guy working on the car can simply grab the line, spray it on and he's done. It's much quicker," explains Abraham, who despite the highs and lows of the detailing industry still loves the business.

Earnings Potential

Although there aren't many hard and fast statistics about the scope and size of the detailing industry, it's easy to do the math to figure out what your potential earnings could be. Let's say you charge $185 for a full interior/exterior detailing. Detail five cars a week, and you'd earn $925 before taxes and expenses. At that pace, your gross revenue would be $48,100 per year. Promote extra services like paintless dent repair, vinyl and leather repair, and paint touch-up, and you can easily get the price of a detailing up to $400 or more. Detail just one extra car a week at $400, and you'd add nearly $21,000 to your gross revenue. That's $69,100 gross for a total of just six cars a week, 52 weeks a year.

Some detailers make even more. One California mobile detailer we know of, who has eight employees, has had annual sales as high as $250,000. On the other hand,

Professional Carwashing & Detailing magazine says the hourly pay for a detailer ranges from $15 to $75, and National Detail Systems, which sells auto detailing and reconditioning systems, estimates an independent detailer can earn $30 to $60 an hour, or $1,000 to $1,500 a week, by detailing two cars a day. The amount you can earn is probably somewhere in the middle, but make no mistake: The sky's the limit for a new detailing professional.

The Opportunities

There are three types of detailing operations: Mobile, express, and site-based. Mobile businesses are the quickest and easiest type to launch, since all you have to do is buy some professional equipment and chemicals, as well as a van or trailer to haul that around in, and take to the road. This is also the most cost-effective way to enter the business, as there's no overhead other than the cost of your professional products and your vehicle, and no mortgage or lease payment. Instead, you work in parking lots, at office complexes, at customers' homes, and possibly in your own garage.

Express detailers often work in carwashes or at auto dealerships. This is a "while you wait" type of business—vehicle owners turn over their keys and wheels so you can do your magic, then get back a sparkling clean vehicle in a set period of time—say, 15 minutes. Although both carwashes and auto dealerships sometimes have their own detailing staff, there are many opportunities to work as a subcontractor at these businesses. And the arrangement is usually pure profit—the owner is usually so thrilled to have someone on site that there's no fee for the use of the space and utilities. This is particularly true of dealerships, where perfect appearance is paramount when it comes to high-priced new and used cars.

Industry experts say that the average price of an express detailing at a carwash is roughly $40, including the carwash. Since the labor rate for the detailing is, at the most, 25 percent and supplies are just a few dollars, profits can be very tidy indeed, considering how little time is necessary to do the work.

Stat Fact

In the more image conscious areas of the country, such as South Florida or Southern California, where a nice looking car "makes a statement" about who you are, it's not uncommon for detailers to charge upwards of $250 for a full detail service.

"I think this is the direction the detailing industry is heading," says Dave Echnoz of 14/69 Carwash Supercenter in Fort Wayne, Indiana. "Twenty minutes, no appointment—it's great for someone who can't be without a car or doesn't want to rent a vehicle."

Fixed-location detailers work out of a building dedicated to detailing. Their overhead is certainly higher than that of a mobile or express detailer, but they have a distinct advantage over the mobile folks: a roof over their heads, so inclement weather that would shut down a mobile detailer is never a problem. With that roof comes a mortgage or lease payment, property taxes, overhead, and myriad other costs. But the trade-off is that site-based detailers can make a lot of money—as much as six figures or more, depending on the size of the operation. Additionally, long-time detailers point to the quality of the more labor intensive detailing versus the "quickie" detailing and stress the added value.

If you're lucky, you might be able to find a detailing shop or service station up for sale that already has all the tools and toys you need, like service bays and professional equipment. If not, you'll have to remodel, but the trade-off is that the finished shop will be exactly the way you want it. Incidentally, some site-based detailers offer express services for customers who are in a hurry. The most common express services are waxing and carpet cleaning.

There's one other type of detailing operation that bears mentioning. Detailing franchises offer another quick way to get into business with a minimum of effort (and cash) upfront. These turnkey operations provide you with an established name, which gives you an instant reputation; resources to help you do business, including advertising and marketing tools and assistance; and sometimes even equipment like mobile trailers. The franchise fees for these operations vary, but they can run tens of thousands of dollars—which can be about as much as establishing your own site-based detail shop would be. For the purposes of this book, we will assume that you are starting your own business from scratch, but just in case you're interested in franchises, you'll find some listed in the Appendix.

The Challenge

Now your mission, should you choose to accept it, is to find the people who have some disposable income they're willing to part with and take pride in their vehicles, as well as automotive professionals who prefer to subcontract the work rather than having detailers on staff. Among the potential prospects are:

- Average Joe (and Josie) consumers who are in love with their cars (carlove.org says 64 percent of car owners talk to their cars and 27 percent give them pet names, so you know they're out there)

- Sports car owners (to whom appearance is everything—including under the hood)

- People who lease cars (since a professional detailing can reduce the chance of incurring ghastly end-of-lease wear-and-tear charges)

- Show car/classic car owners/car buffs who show off their vehicles for love . . . and money

- New and used vehicle dealerships (the pace can be grueling and the work doesn't always pay top dollar, but there's usually a lot of work for a new detailer)

▲

- People who are selling their own cars in the local classifieds (currently a huge untapped market)
- RV dealerships and their customers (still another gold mine of possibilities)
- Automotive centers like auto malls
- Carwashes (usually as an express detailing operation)
- Auto repair shops (including collision shops)
- Limousine companies
- Hotels with concierge service that might want to offer detailing as a premium service to guests
- Gas stations/garages that offer complete automotive services

Other prospects include boat and airplane owners (gotta look "fly" as they cast off or taxi away from the terminal) and railroad companies (don't worry—Meguiar's has you covered with the appropriate train polish). Many detailers start with cars, then segue into other types of vehicle detailing as a way to keep busy when the weather is poor. This type of detailing work is also a wide open market for entrepreneurs.

So are you ready to clean up in this promising industry? Great. Then turn the page so we can get your new business cranked up.

The Well-Oiled Business Machine

Although there's a lot more to starting a detailing business than buying a bunch of powerful car toys (e.g., buffers and extractors) and playing with professional-grade products, we know you're dying to start dyeing and polishing. So this chapter will focus on the different maintenance and restoration services a detailer can provide, as well as the day-to-day functions involved in running the business.

One of the first things you should do in the process of setting up a detailing business is to determine exactly which services you'd like to perform. If you've been an amateur detailer ever since you got your first set of wheels, you already have a pretty good idea what a detailer does, as well as how long it takes to do it. But just in case you've never detailed a car before, or it's been years since you've had time to pamper your own chrome cruiser, let's take a look at the many services a detailer can offer.

Cleaning Up

Among the basic exterior detailing services are:

- Hand wash (with particular attention to tree sap, bug remains, bird droppings, and rail dust)
- Hand dry, usually with chamois or another soft, lint-free cloth
- Claying to remove all surface contaminants from the paint after the vehicle is washed
- Hand application of wax or sealant
- Application of wax using an orbital buffer
- Window and exterior mirror cleaning
- Trim and tire dressing application and polishing
- Wheel/rim waxing

Regular interior detailing services include:

- Floor and seat vacuuming (including vacuuming with a crevice tool for deep penetration)
- Floor and seat shampooing
- Cleaning and dressing of dashboard, door panels, and center console
- Vent, kick panel, pedal, doorjamb, and ashtray cleaning
- Floor mat vacuuming and steam cleaning
- Headliner cleaning
- Leather seat and trim cleaning and conditioning
- Vinyl seat cleaning and dressing
- Window and mirror cleaning and polishing

It's not necessary to offer every service on these lists as part of your regular interior or exterior detailing. Rather, you'll need to create the right combination of services that will maximize your profits while keeping labor costs firmly in check. For instance, you may find it's sufficient to vacuum a vehicle's interior thoroughly rather than shampooing the carpet as part of every interior detailing. Or perhaps steam cleaning is enough to freshen up a vehicle's interior. You'll need to make that determination based on factors like local weather conditions and the expectations created by your competition.

Detailers typically offer a wide range of additional services as a way to earn more money per vehicle. Often, these upgraded services are part of special packages concocted by the detailer to address different maintenance and restoration issues. Among these upgraded services are:

- Engine detailing (including degreasing and washing the engine, doorjambs, and hoses; cleaning under the hood and motor compartment)
- Trunk cleaning (vacuuming the interior, washing the jambs)
- Undercarriage detailing (removing road salt, dirt, and tar from the underbody and wheels, painting of wheels, applying undercoat)
- Scotchguard®, UV sealer applications for upholstery
- Carpeting and upholstery dyeing
- Trim and instrumentation repairs
- Odor removal and deodorizing
- Ozone odor removal
- Exterior Teflon® sealant
- Compounding and polishing to remove oxidation, scratches, scuffs, swirl marks, minor scratches, water spots, and stains
- Convertible top care
- Windshield wiper replacement

Finally, there are several specialty add-on services you can offer that will really beef up your bottom line. These services not only will maximize the amount you can earn on every vehicle you detail, but also they can be very lucrative profit centers in themselves. However, some of these services require hands-on training before you go to town on someone's vehicle so you don't inadvertently cause damage. Among the popular add-ons are:

- Custom paint touch-up, chip and scratch repair
- Black trim restoration
- Carpet and upholstery dyeing
- Vinyl and leather repair
- Windshield repair and tinting
- Paintless dent repair
- Overspray or cement removal

Obviously, not every detailer will be able to offer all these services. In fact, the prospect of offering so many services can be downright scary for

> **Tip...**
>
> **Smart Tip**
> Using the proper equipment and chemicals will help you complete your work more efficiently and in less time. Case in point: Lint-free towels or chamois may cost more, but you won't have to worry about fibers clinging to a vehicle's paint finish when you're ready to start waxing.

some people. Often the decision about what you'll offer will be dependent on the size of your facility and whether you can afford the equipment when you start out. It may also be dependant upon what you are good at or what specialties have been added by the people you have hired. On the mobile side, you might have to limit your services simply because you have to carry every piece of equipment and every product you'll need with you on the road, including water tanks, spray equipment, and other devices. Some of the specialty services require equipment that's just not portable enough for a mobile detailer who's already carrying so much stuff—unless, of course, you plan to invest in a really big rig.

> ## Smart Tip
> Tip...
>
> There's no need to be secretive when you're collecting information about your competitors. With 130 million cars on the road, there's plenty of business to go around, and most competitors will welcome the opportunity to exchange ideas and war stories with another professional in the field.

Sometimes being "the best" in town in several highly requested detailing areas is better for marketing and drawing customers than trying to offer everything possible.

Although it's not unusual for detailers to offer à la carte services, especially if the market is smaller and more price-sensitive, it's actually more common to offer packages of services as a way to make vehicles—and your bottom line—really shine. The cost for a package is usually less than the cost of the individual services combined, which is perceived as a better value by the customer. For instance, a complete bumper-to-fender detailing package might include hand wash and wax services, from deep cleaning of interior surfaces to engine and trunk detailing. A buffing and compounding package to remove surface scratches and swirls would start with a full wash and wax followed by custom paint chip and scratch repair.

A package is beneficial to you because you can spend more time working on one car than taking time to handle payment and paperwork for one vehicle while you await to get started on the next one. In essence you can do more on one car in an hour than you can on two cars with the time gap in between, talking to the customers, etc., etc. And that's not to mention if one person scheduled for 3:00 shows up at 3:15.

Here's an example of what a full detail package might include:

- Hand washing and drying
- Claying, buffing, and waxing
- Deep cleaning (shampooing) of interior surfaces, including carpets and mats, and leather or vinyl upholstery conditioning
- Dressing of tires/wheels cleaned and polished
- Engine compartment and trunk detailing

For a package like this, you could charge anywhere from $125 to $235, depending on what your market will bear. In large metro markets, like Los Angeles, you could charge even more. Naturally, oversized vehicles like SUVs and trucks would also cost more in any market. One detailer we know charges 20 percent more for oversized vehicles.

So how do you know what to include in your packages? One way to make a determination is to check out what your competitors are doing. Certainly, some services beyond basic washing and waxing should be standard in your packages, like carpet and mat cleaning and interior dressing. But you can make a splash among the other detailers in your area by offering a service that's not commonly available, such as engine compartment cleaning. Just be sure you know what you're getting into if that's your choice. With all the electronic equipment packed under the hood these days, engine cleaning isn't easy, particularly if you have large hands that can't easily slip between the hoses and hardware. But the scratches and scrapes will be worth it if adding this kind of service will bring more customers to your door or more calls for your mobile service—if you can complete such jobs in a reasonable amount of time. Remember, time equals money and whatever you choose to add, if it is taking more time than it is worth in dollars, than you may be costing yourself more business. Calculate the time factor into your decision to add special services.

Kevin Traver, owner of Perfect Auto Finish (www.perfectautofinish.com) in Roselle, Illinois offers four packages starting with a complete interior cleaning for $125, which includes hand wash, interior vacuuming, interior steam cleaning, fabric seats steam cleaned and scotch guarded, plastic cleaned, trunk compartment cleaned, and more, and going up to a an ultimate, complete interior and exterior package for $225. Like most detailers, Traver, who's been in business for eight years, finds that it's easier for customers to choose among a few packages than try to sort through a long a la carte menu.

Detailers who have been in the business awhile recommend keeping your detailing menu simple. Offering choices like a full interior/exterior detail, an interior-only detail, a wash and exterior-only detail, and maybe express services like waxing alone or carpet cleaning alone are more than enough options when you start out. Because not all services (like claying) are familiar to customers, you should create a service menu brochure that gives the components of each package and explains the more mysterious services. The brochure can also be used as a direct-mail piece to upsell your services. Simply hand one to your customer when you take his/her keys and mention the full range of services you offer. You also should be sure to display a quantity of these service brochures in a plastic holder on your service counter or give one to mobile customers at the same time you give them a receipt. A wall menu, not unlike ones you see at the fast food restaurants, can also be valuable with a few packages and brief descriptions, plus prices of course.

You'll find information about creating and printing a brochure in Chapter 10, but in the meantime, you can check out the sample brochure on page 14.

To help you make sure you're covering all your bases when you're detailing a car, use the Detailing Checklist on page 15.

Sample Brochure

1. *Cover*

Great Lakes Automotive Detailing

The automotive reconditioning
and restoration experts

(555) 555-0000

2. *Back*

*Your vehicle can look
like new again!*

*We know you take pride in your car,
SUV, van, or truck. But Michigan
weather can really take a toll on your
prized wheels. So let the automotive
experts at Great Lakes Automotive
Detailing restore the showroom shine
with a professional interior and exterior detailing.*

*Besides making your vehicle look
great, detailing also is a wise investment. It can prolong the life and
beauty of your vehicle. It can increase
the value of a vehicle you're planning
to sell. It even can minimize end-of-
lease charges you might incur when
you turn in your leased vehicle.*

**Trust the experts at
Great Lakes Automotive Detailing**

*The pros at Great Lakes Automotive
Detailing will maintain, recondition,
and restore your vehicle using professional-grade equipment and high-
quality products. To make your vehicle
shine like new again, call today for an
appointment.*

(555) 555-0000

Great Lakes Automotive Detailing
5555 Jefferson Avenue
St. Clair Shores, Michigan 48051

(555) 555-0000
www.greatlakesdetailing.com
info@greatlakesdetailing.com

3. *Inside*

Detailing Services

- Hand wash and dry, buff, and wax—$39.95
- Interior vacuuming, plastic and vinyl/leather cleaning, conditioning—$29.95
- Carpet/mat steam cleaning and conditioning—$39.95
- Scotchguarding (upholstery, carpeting)—$29.95
- Engine cleaning (grease removed, engine compartment cleaned)—$49.95
- Odor removal—$35
- Deodorizing—$25
- Paintless dent repair—from $50
- Paint touch-up, scratch repair—from $50
- Vinyl/leather repair—from $25

Detailing Packages

Interior Detailing—From $125
- Hand wash
- Interior vacuum
- Fabric seats, carpets, mats steam cleaned
- Leather or vinyl seats cleaned and conditioned
- Dash, console, trim, vents, pedals cleaned and protected
- Windows cleaned
- Doorjambs cleaned

Exterior Detailing—From $150
- Hand washing and old wax removal
- Clay bar dirt/grit removal
- Buffing and waxing of painted surfaces
- Tires dressed
- Wheels polished, wheel wells protected
- Windows and mirrors cleaned
- Engine compartment cleaned

*Note: All prices are approximate and may vary
depending on the size and condition of the vehicle.*

Deluxe Detailing—From $195
Your best value!

Includes all interior and exterior services
listed at left, plus carpet and upholstery
shampooing and Scotchguarding,
engine cleaning and degreasing, and
trunk and jamb cleaning.

*Service hours
Monday-Friday
10 A.M. to 5 P.M.
Saturday
by appointment*

Pickup and delivery service available
with 24-hour notice. Visa, MasterCard,
and American Express accepted.

Great Lakes Automotive Detailing
5555 Jefferson Avenue
St. Clair Shores, Michigan 48051

(555) 555-0000
www.greatlakesdetailing.com
info@greatlakesdetailing.com

Detailing Checklist

A detailing service includes cleaning and inspection of all the following areas:

Engine compartment
- ❑ Inside hood
- ❑ Engine and hoses
- ❑ Outer lip and water channel
- ❑ All painted surfaces

Exterior
- ❑ All painted surfaces polished
- ❑ All painted surfaces lusterized
- ❑ Vinyl or cloth top
- ❑ Front, side, and rear lights
- ❑ Front grill
- ❑ Front air dam
- ❑ Front and rear bumpers
- ❑ Doorjambs and hinges
- ❑ Gas tank compartment
- ❑ Wheel well edge and moldings
- ❑ Wheel well compartment
- ❑ Wheels
- ❑ Tires
- ❑ Rocker panels
- ❑ Chrome polished (door edges, bumpers, trim)
- ❑ Weather stripping
- ❑ Body side moldings
- ❑ Side mirrors
- ❑ License plate(s)
- ❑ Tailpipe
- ❑ Pinstripes (free from wax deposits)
- ❑ Windows (including edges)
- ❑ Window trim

Protective coatings applied to:
- ❑ Tires (tire dressing)
- ❑ Vinyl roof (vinyl dressing)

- ❑ Rubber bumpers, side moldings, weather stripping
- ❑ Dashboard
- ❑ Leather
- ❑ Wood trim
- ❑ Vinyl seats and door panels

Interior
- ❑ Floor mats
- ❑ Pedals, gearshift
- ❑ Headliner
- ❑ Dashboard
- ❑ Instrument panel (vents, knobs, gauges)
- ❑ Sun visors
- ❑ Interior mirrors
- ❑ Steering wheel
- ❑ Glove box, side storage boxes
- ❑ Center console
- ❑ Ashtrays (front and rear)
- ❑ Carpet/floor
- ❑ Seats
- ❑ Seat tracks
- ❑ Door panels
- ❑ Rear shelf
- ❑ All chrome/plastic trim
- ❑ Sunroof tracks
- ❑ Window trim
- ❑ Windows (including edges)

Trunk compartment
- ❑ Inside lid
- ❑ Interior carpet or vinyl
- ❑ Outer lip and water channel
- ❑ Place floor mats into trunk
- ❑ Replace items removed from vehicle

Comments:_____
_____
_____
_____

Technicians:_____ Final inspection by: _____

Courtesy of Karen Duncan

Pricing Your Services

Setting appropriate prices for the work you do is always a difficult task for a new business owner. Price your services too high, and you'll limit the number of people who can afford them; price them too low, and you'll limit your profit potential and possibly give your customers the perception that you're not as professional or competent as the guy (or gal) down the street.

"Selling by price alone will put a detailer out of business because there is always someone who will sell cheaper," warns detailing industry expert R. L. "Bud" Abraham, who is also owner of Detail Plus Car Appearance Systems in Portland, Oregon. "As a rule of thumb, a detail shop should have a profit margin of at least twenty percent after all expenses, including the detailer's salary, and benefits."

To illustrate how pricing works, you need to start with an hourly rate that is in line with the market. This is what you get for your time. Unfortunately, the bulk of this

The Price Is Right

The price you can charge for detailing services varies widely across the country, so here are some ranges for the most popular auto detailing services that you can refer to when you set your own prices:

- Full detail: $150–$225 (or more for luxury vehicles)
- Express detail: $40–$75
- Hand wash and vacuum: $25–$40
- Interior shampooing and cleaning: $80–$100
- Machine polish and wax: $100–$150
- Carpet dyeing: $75–$150
- Black trim restoration: $25–$100
- Paint touch-up: $75–$200
- Paintless dent repair: $75–$150 per dent
- Windshield repair: $25–$80
- Window tinting: $100 and up
- Leather and vinyl repair: $25–$75
- Overspray or cement removal: $125-$175

money goes back into running the business and not into your pocket. After adding on expenses, you want to see a 20 percent, or perhaps 25 percent profit.

So, assuming you want to make $30 an hour for a job and it takes you three hours, that's $90. Now add on the expenses (including soap, polishes, and the electricity to run your equipment). Let's say this is $15—always estimate a little bit higher since it's hard to judge how much electricity was used or how many towels may have been used (unless you have the time to count). Now, you're up to $105. However, to see a profit, you now want to add 20 or 25 percent, depending on what you can get in your market. At 20 percent you would tack on $21 and at 25 percent, you would tack on $26. Adding this to your $105, you would be charging between $126 to $131, which you could round off to $125 to $130.

Smart Tip

Give customers a price range, rather than a set price. This way, if the customer wasn't very honest by phone or email about the condition of the car, you can charge higher for your additional hours, and if the car looks as anticipated, you can go by the lower end rate.

This is one way to determine your prices, which works particularly well for a mobile detailer. The same formula would work if you have employees, but of course you would pay them less per hour, so your profit would be higher. But if you decide to offer benefits, you'll have to figure in that amount, too.

If you operate out of a fixed facility, you'll have to take into account operating expenses like your mortgage or lease and utilities when you set your prices. Chapter 13 talks about how to figure operating expenses and has an income and operating expenses worksheet you can use to help calculate your costs so you can adjust your price schedule as necessary. Just as a heads up: You can reasonably assume that your overhead will be from 40 to 50 percent of your labor and materials cost.

Need help calculating a reasonable hourly rate? Here's a simple formula. Let's assume you're a mobile detailer and you want to make $40,000 per year.

$40,000 ÷ 52 weeks = $769 per week

$769 ÷ 48 (8 hours per day x 6 days per week) = $16 per hour

Add a 20 percent profit margin ($3.20) = $19.20 per hour

Then average in your supply costs, loan repayment, etc., and you'll have a good handle on how much you need to earn to make ends meet and put some money in the bank. You might want to start out, before picking a number like $40,000, by determining what you need to earn in a year to make ends meet. Then use the above means of calculations to determine an hourly rate. While you could certainly work 50 hours a week, it's best to estimate a lower number since you cannot be sure you will have enough paying work for all of those hours. Don't forget that some of your work hours will be doing paperwork, ordering supplies, etc., etc. These are not hours in which you are bringing in any money.

"A lot of detailers don't charge enough because they don't look at how much it costs to do business," says Karen Duncan of Union Park Appearance Care Center in Wilmington, Delaware, who also owned a detailing business called We Love Your Car for 15 years before a natural disaster put her out of business in 2003. "I put a lot of thought into my prices based on my expenses and how long it took to do the work. I ended up being higher priced than most detailers, but I had a good following and a good business," she says.

Other detailers don't charge enough because they quote prices over the phone without ever seeing the vehicle, according to Tom Schurmann, former owner of Masterfinish and current owner of Professional Detailing Systems in Lakewood, Colorado, who sold his detailing business after 32 years so he could try his hand at selling his detailing system to other detailers. "We never quoted or printed hard prices. I explained that to do the best job I had to see what the vehicle needed," Schurmann says. "If pushed, I would quote a ballpark spread, which seemed to make people want to stop by to see if they qualified for the low side. Some guys will go out on a limb and offer a $99 special over the phone, and then the customer turns up with a 15-passenger van that was in a field with cattle living in it."

Rennie Doyle, of Perfect Auto finish with six locations nationwide, says that a simple menu can be very effective. "Our menu is much like that of the popular West Coast fast food chain, In & Out Burger. They have a simple menu with about five items. Using that same principle, we designed our menu to have a few packages," explains Doyle. While catering to a high-end clientele, Doyle adds that they also offer Express Detailing, which runs from $89 to $120. "We spot clean the carpets, wipe everything down, vacuum, wash, and use a spray wax instead of using paste or liquid. It's still very high quality, but a spray application takes about 10 percent of the time, allowing us to charge less money for man hours."

Parts and Labor

Despite the fact that you'll have a finite number of tasks to perform as a detailer, you'll soon find out you'll have a lot of variety in your day-to-day business life. To begin with, you'll probably spend a fair amount of time on the telephone every day, booking appointments, ordering supplies, and talking to salespeople. If you're mobile, you'll also have to make up a work schedule so you know exactly where you're supposed to be at any given time of the day. If you have employees, you'll have to coordinate their schedules, referee when those schedules (or the employees themselves) collide, hold training sessions, hire new people to replace those who leave, visit high school career day events to troll for new prospects, and so on. You'll also have to deal with building and detailing equipment maintenance (including detailing your own equipment so it's a shining example of the good work you do). You'll be in charge of money management, customer service, and the complaint department. Finally, it'll be your job to keep the work area clean, uncluttered, and swept up, and the bathrooms scrupulously clean.

Smart Tip

To increase retail sales, try giving your customers a sample bottle of one or more of the products you use on their vehicles. If they like it, they'll be back to buy more. If they don't, the least you've done is to build customer goodwill, which in turn may result in positive word-of-mouth advertising.

Sounds like a lot for one person to do, doesn't it? Well, it is—and it's the reason why some detailers choose to hire an assistant manager to help with the chores. We'll talk more about personnel, including how to find qualified help, in Chapter 8. In the meantime, you'll need a weekly or monthly planner to help you keep appointments and activities straight and on schedule. You can pick one up at any office supply store. You can also consider using a PC- or Mac-based calendar or scheduler program instead. There are plenty of organizing and scheduling software programs available, not specifically for auto detailing, but for business in general. Of course you could always just make a list of appointments on your Excel word program or even by hand in a notebook. The point is, you need a system of maintaining your ongoing schedule—one that works best for you.

Tales from the (Store) Front

Whether you're going mobile or facility-based, you should make a decision about your hours of operation early on. Mobile detailers generally work during regular business hours because many of them do their stuff in the parking lots of office buildings while their customers are at work. Having Saturday hours may also be a good idea if you have clients who prefer a house call. In addition, if the weather foils your detailing schedule during the week, you can pick up the slack on the weekend. Standard business hours of 9 A.M. to 5 P.M. should be fine given the clientele you're likely to have, but of course when the days are longer, there's no reason why you can't detail in the evening if you're so inclined. Just pick your locations carefully—no matter how safe an area is, it's not a good idea to be out in the middle of nowhere with no one around late at night, especially when your attention is on your work and not the area around you.

The ideal place to do your mobile magic is in a temporary location. The owner of Ultimate Reflections in San Antonio has an arrangement with administrators at two hospitals to detail cars right on site. In both cases, the arrangements were made after cardiologists at the health-care facilities asked him to detail their cars at the hospital, and he doesn't pay anything for the use of the spaces, which are under cover. He simply

▲

Smart Tip

Tip...

Put the finishing touch on a professional detail job with a complimentary license plate touch-up. Use touch-up paint that matches your state's license plate color, then seal it with clearcoat spray. It only takes about ten minutes, and the customer will definitely be impressed with your extra effort.

washes and waxes the hospital security vehicles on a regular basis in exchange for permission to detail physicians' cars on site.

Site-based detailers are more likely to have standard retail business hours of 9 A.M. to 6 P.M., six days a week, or perhaps shorter hours on Saturdays. Some detailers start their work at 7 A.M. so that customers can drop off their cars before going to work. Others stay open until 7 P.M. so that customers can pick up their cars on the way home. The point is, know your customers, your neighborhood and try to have some hours that do not correspond to the typical 9 to 5 workday.

Tom Schurmann of Professional Detailing Systems in Lakewood, Colorado, a detailer for more than 30 years, says that's not always the best way to go. When he first started his business, he did a lot of dealer work on what he calls the "burnout schedule:" daily from 8 A.M. to 6 P.M. and Saturdays from 8:30 A.M. to 5 P.M. After a dozen years, his retail business was strong enough that he could start dropping the dealership work, which he said didn't pay as much as retail work anyway. Eventually, he dropped dealership work altogether.

"Retail only was the most relaxed schedule—8 to 5 and Saturdays by appointment," Schurmann says. "Instead of detailing 17 or more cars a day, we went down to three cars a day, and we ended up making more money doing less. It was a wonderful, enjoyable time."

Padding with Products

How would you like to make extra money each month with very little effort? Then plan to offer a carefully selected assortment of consumer detailing products. Selling products is a great means of generating additional business for all types of service industries.

According to merchandising experts, retail products can make your profits grow significantly with minimal effort. All you have to do is buy extra products from your supplier—like polishes and waxes, shampoos and chamois—mark them up for retail sale, and display them on shelving in your waiting area (preferably behind the counter where they can't walk away when your attention is elsewhere). Then remember to suggest certain products to your customers as they're cashing out. (This also works for mobile detailers, of course—you just keep a supply in your vehicle.) A smooth sales pitch might go something like this: "If you want to preserve that nice shine on your dashboard between detailings, you can use XYZ Product, which is what I just used. I've got it in stock for just $3.95 for a six-month supply if you're interested."

Card 'Em

Need one more idea for add-on sales? Then try gift cards, or gift certificates, which have become a very hot commodity in the retail sales world. All kinds of businesses, from bookstores and restaurants to hair salons and even movie theaters, have been selling gift cards with great success. The idea of the card is that it fits nicely into a wallet and can be easily redeemed (in most cases) electronically, like a credit card, leaving the individual with a balance on the card if they do not spend the entire amount. You can also trade off with other local merchants and sell each other's cards along with your own. This gives your business added exposure in another business location.

Gift cards, or certificates, are great because they can bring in a lot of cash for a very small investment. The downside is, they're probably going to be redeemed at some point, which technically means you'll be providing services for nothing at that time. For that reason, you might want to tuck away your gift certificate cash in a separate account that you can draw against whenever a card or certificate is redeemed. Don't forget to sell extras. These customers are getting something for nothing (since the card was a gift). Therefore, they are the best sales targets for some products, since that's the only money they are spending. In fact, many of these customers are anxious to spend some money while they wait.

"We found that gift certificates were very lucrative," Schurmann says. "It was money upfront, and most recipients had never had a detail before. With our quality work, we gained a new customer for life. We also found it very easy to point out and sell upgraded packages to get them into our six-month return program."

Weather Beaters

As the saying goes, into every life a little rain must fall—but inclement weather can be a business buster for the detailer. The minute the forecast calls for rain, snow, ice, or even high winds that can kick up dust devils, the cancellations will pour in because no one is going to spend big bucks on a detailing job that may be ruined the minute they drive out of your shop.

Mobile detailers know better than anyone that business grinds to a halt on bad-weather days. It's possible to erect a canopy over your work area and the vehicle you're pampering during a sudden downpour, but such a tent isn't meant for anything other than temporary

Smart Tip

Tip...

Consider offering maintenance contracts. With a maintenance program you will wash someone's car a certain number of times a month; perhaps twice and wax it once, along with other features. You can offer a few programs. This will provide you with money up-front to help with cash flow and provide you with steady customers.

shelter. So you have no recourse except to shut down for the day... or the week.

Mobile detailers often use their downtime to catch up on paperwork, order supplies, and read emails. But there are other moneymaking operations you can undertake to make the time off more profitable. For instance, some detailers expand into the electronic accessories installation market to beef up sales. Having a steady stream of alarms, audio systems (including satellite radio), remote starters, and neon license plates available and promoting this line of services as an offshoot of your regular detailing business can help offset weather downtimes. Of course, these services also decrease the amount of time you can spend detailing, so be sure not to take on more than you can handle.

Detailers like Mike Myers of Gem Auto Appearance Center in Waldorf, Maryland, have diversified as a way to stay busy. Myers went from a mobile operation to a fixed-location to aircraft and boat detailing. "With the weather here in the East, you could struggle in the winter months. I've had years when I wasn't fit to talk to. I'd get home and my wife would slide my food under the door. I ate a lot of pancakes," he says, laughing.

Prentice St. Clair, a San Diego detailing industry expert and owner of Detail in Progress, recommended in an issue of *Professional Carwashing & Detailing* magazine that establishing yourself as an expert who can recondition all types of surfaces is a great way to get add-on business that can carry you through downtimes. "You can create a poster for your shop and do a special mailing once a year titled, 'Did you know that we can...,' followed by a list of special cleaning situations you can handle with the chemicals and equipment you already have," St. Clair says. "These appointments could easily be set up after hours, on typically slow days, or during inclement weather."

Among the ways you can use your knowledge of detailing chemicals and equipment are to restore lawn and patio furniture, to pressure-wash vinyl siding, to remove stains from driveways and sidewalks, and to polish and wax garage floors.

Inclement weather is bad enough, but there's another type of weather condition that can have a devastating effect on a detailer's business. Drought conditions that result in water restrictions can effectively close down a detailing business—perhaps for good—because the owner must abide by the same restrictions as the rest of the community. And don't expect anyone except perhaps your most loyal customers to wait for you until the drought breaks. They're more likely to head for the nearest carwash, since carwashes are sometimes not required to curtail their water usage during a drought. There's nothing much you can do during a drought except pray for rain and look for some other work, including the add-ons mentioned earlier. Better yet, establish a relationship with a carwash to provide detailing services, as discussed in Chapter 1, so you'll have work to carry you through the dry spells.

Doing Your Homework:
Your Guide to Market Research

If one day you decided that your tolerance for snowstorms and Arctic temperatures was way past its expiration date and a warmer climate was essential for ongoing good mental health, would you just call up a real estate broker and tell her to pick out a charming little bungalow for you in the tropical paradise of her choice? Probably not. You're more likely to take a more organized approach to house hunting, including specifying the type and size of abode you need and taking into consideration practical matters like proximity to schools and shopping and the availability of enough fast-food joints to keep your kids happy until they can vote.

This is the same kind of informed decision-making process you must use when you're considering where to set up shop for your detailing business (even if your "shop" is a mobile rig). You absolutely must scout out your target market to determine whether there's even a need for your services, as well as the likelihood that someone will be willing and able to pay for them. The way to cue yourself in on that essential data is by conducting some market research.

Market research involves tasks like identifying and understanding the needs of promising market segments (a fancy term for customers), and differentiating your services from those of your competition. Remember the age-old real estate adage, location, location, location? Well, market research, research, research is the determining factor when choosing that important location. In short, it's a crucial part of the successful launch of a new business. So here's a crash course on how to make short work of basic market research so you can get down to doing the work you like best—detailing really cool cars (and maybe even some clunkers) and making trunkfuls of money.

Smart Tip

A lot of detailers go after the luxury-car market, but there are just as many opportunities in the consumer market, particularly when it comes to people who want to make their leased cars look like new before turning them in. Specializing in this segment alone can bring great financial rewards.

Warning! Warning!

We interrupt this chapter to bring you a public service announcement that is crucial to the health of your business, both in its infancy and its old age: You must not bypass market research if you're serious about success. Now, we understand that you'll be tempted to rush out and buy an extractor, chamois, and buffing compound and start putting that spit shine on vehicles in need of pampering. But you cannot make money if you're marketing to the wrong audience, no matter how enthusiastic you are or how many car toys you have.

Market research will help you

- identify the people who are most likely to want and need your services.
- identify businesses with which you can align yourself
- determine whether the location in which you want to open your business can actually sustain the business.

- discover useful information that can help you avoid big problems down the road that could curtail or close your business.

Luckily, you can do your own market research armed with just a few simple tools, and it doesn't have to cost you an arm and a leg.

Rev It Up

The first thing you need to determine is the specific characteristics that influence the buying habits of your potential customers. These characteristics, known as demographics, will help you figure out how to position your service best. Here's an example: Let's say you've decided to work out of an actual facility. You find a place you love—an inexpensive, one-bay unit near an auto mall in a Big Ten college town with 100,000 people (a large percentage of whom are students). On the outskirts of Universityville are a number of middle-class "bedroom communities" with 1920s Craftsman-style bungalows. The area is hip, trendy, and peopled by young families with one wage earner and no day-care expenses.

The question is: Can your detailing business survive there? Let's decide by taking a look at the Demographic Analysis chart of this hypothetical geographical area.

First, being near an auto mall means you may be able to strike up a deal with the owner or general manager of the mall to detail their new or used cars. Such an arrangement can make this a very profitable location. In addition, you will typically find that many college students with their first automobiles, and a penchant for attracting the opposite sex, want a good looking car, so they will splurge on occasion for some buffing and waxing. The key is evaluating a location and the people that could be your customers. Is there enough potential business to make your detailing shop work? In this case, there may be, but you'll need to first see if you can build an arrangement with the auto mall.

So who is likely to be your best customer, besides those auto dealers? Probably baby boomers, who love having nice cars but don't have the time to care for them... auto enthusiasts who garage their prized rides during inclement weather and would swoon at the sight of a swirl mark... classic car collectors who show their vehicles in parades... people who want to spiff up their vehicles before trading them or turning them in at the end of a lease... and the list goes on.

Demographics include several areas of interest. You need to look at income level,

Dollar Stretcher

Be sure to check out the U.S. Census Bureau's website at www.census.gov when you start your market research. This site has a wealth of demographic information organized by state and county that can be very useful when investigating the demographics of your target market. The information can be instantly downloaded at no charge.

occupations, gender, education, and other factors to get an overall picture of the geographic area. (See a sample Demographic Analysis on page 27.) It's important, however, not to get overly caught up in making generalizations about these numbers because they don't always tell you the whole story. For example, someone with a lower level of income and less education will still, very likely, be concerned more about the look of their car in, or around, the Los Angeles area where car use is very high and the look of a car can demonstrate a level of status and taste. In Manhattan, however, you may find an area where you have individuals with high income and a high level of education, but park their cars in garages, rarely use them, and rate the look of their cars much farther down on their list of priorities. Therefore, you cannot paint accurate pictures based on generalities. Instead, factor in a realistic profile of the wants and needs of the demographic group as it relates to their cars.

Some factors are true across the board. For example, no one wants to open what is essentially a luxury-based business in a town where the economy is in a downturn. If, for example, you find a town where one industry employs most of the people and that industry is in flux, you may opt to look elsewhere.

Finally, you'll want to look at overall population since a detailing business relies on volume and repeat business. A city with a high-density business district is going to be a better choice for the business than a rural community with one gas station and a post office. The Census Bureau and the local chamber of commerce are good sources of population data.

Conducting Market Research

This isn't as hard as you might think. To begin with, there are two types of research: primary research, which is gathered firsthand from people in response to written or verbal questions, and secondary research, which is collected by studying information gathered by other people. Both are helpful for detailers like you who are trying to build a business strategy.

Primary Research

There are three types of primary research that are useful for detailers.

1. **Historical**. Study past data to understand your market, such as business records to find out the failure rate for automotive businesses and detailers in general in your market. Remember, as in investing, past information does not always predict the future. Therefore, you need to look beyond this one aspect of your research.

2. **Observational**. Watch your potential customers to determine their buying behavior (such as camping out near an established detailer to observe what

Demographic Analysis	
Age:	Many of the inhabitants are young and this is a plus since young people are more often concerned about the look of their vehicles.
Education:	Many have at least some college education.
Gender:	There are probably more female than male students. The Census Bureau says 55 percent of college students are female. This, however, is a generalization and is an example of a number that could mislead you completely. You would want to look more closely at these specific colleges. If there are more males in these schools, that would be to your advantage, since males are typically more interested in detailing their cars than females.
Occupation:	On one hand, you have many students who are not working. On the other hand, universities employ numerous people at all income levels. Income, therefore, is probably not going to be a major factor.
Income:	Look at this in terms of the local economy. If income levels are low but expenses are also low, then it leaves people with disposable income, and visa versa. The only time income becomes a problem is when income levels are below the standard of living in the area, or inflation is particularly high. That's when middle and lower income families need to tighten their belts and luxuries (such as detailing) take a hit.
Geographic:	Consider the above Los Angeles/New York City comparison. What is the status of a good-looking car in a geographic region? College students will spend the money from a part time job on their cars because it's important to look "cool." Of course, if you are in a location that is hit with hard winters and nobody gets to drive fashionable looking cars for six months, that is also a key factor. You might look at the number of car shows in the area and attendance figures to get a feel for how many car enthusiasts are around. If possible, check with some of the leading car magazines and see if they have a high number of subscribers, or sell a significant number of newsstand copies of their magazines in this area. The level of interest in cars in a geographic region is important.

types of people—i.e., age, gender, etc.—use the business). Tom Schurmann of Lakewood, Colorado, used this method before opening his first shop, Masterfinish, in 1979. He studied the market for months. He took pictures of competitors' shops and then went into those shops and asked for quotes. He also recorded his experiences and observations about the location and its appearance, attitude, cleanliness, professionalism, and so on. Then he carefully reviewed his findings and determined that he could do a better job … and a new detailer was born.

3. **Survey**. Ask prospects what they're looking for in a detailer through the use of direct-mail pieces, telemarketing, and personal interviews. Of the three, direct-mail surveys are the most cost-effective and least time-consuming tool for gathering information for a new business owner on a tight budget. Plus, they're relatively inexpensive to produce. If, however, you can provide a small incentive for surveying people at a mall or other public location, you can typically get the most accurate data. After all, mailings could be filled out haphazardly or by the twelve-year-old son of the homeowner.

Questionnaires can be a little tricky to write. You'll want to make sure your questions are short and to the point. They should mostly be open-ended, which means they can't be answered with just a "yes" or "no." For example, a simple question like "Would you be interested in mobile detailing done right at your home or office?" isn't very useful because if a respondent says "No," you haven't learned anything; you don't know the reasons behind the answer. A better question might be "How many times last year did you have your vehicle detailed?" Then follow up with questions like "If never, why not?" and "Which services did you like best?"

It's important that you do not ask too many questions and that you do not seek out personally identifiable information in an age where people are very concerned about identity theft.

If you need help phrasing your questions for maximum impact, try getting help from the business school at your local university or look at other survey samples used by existing businesses. According to David Williams, Ph.D., a professor in the marketing department in the School of Business at Wayne State University in Detroit, a marketing professor might be

> ### Smart Tip
> **Tip…**
>
> When doing a market survey, first try to narrow your list down to targeted individuals, or those who own cars and are within the age range most likely to even consider detailing. Having bus commuters filling out your survey gives you junk data.
>
> Be sure your test panel is large enough to yield a statistically significant sample. According to industry experts, direct-mail response rates average just 10 percent, which would mean only 30 are returned out of 300. To obtain enough useful data, make your test panel as large as your budget will allow.

willing to draft your questionnaire for $500 to $1,000, which is a bargain compared to what a marketing firm would charge. Alternatively, he or she may assign your questionnaire as a class project and pass along the results to you free of charge.

If you'd like to try creating your own survey, check out the market research questionnaire postcard, which you can use as a guideline, which starts on pages 31. You might insert this survey postcard in a direct mailing to prospective customers, complete with a market research letter like the one on page 33.

Once your questionnaire has been developed, the next step is to mail it out to a random sampling of consumers in your area. There are a number of companies and organizations that sell their mailing list to business owners like you for a nominal fee. These lists are usually organized in categories by demographics, so you can pick, for instance, heads of household aged 45 and up or couples with combined annual incomes of more than $75,000. Local homeowners' associations, list brokers, and even daily newspapers in major metropolitan areas are all good sources of mailing lists, as are the corporate offices of trade show companies, which often compile the names of attendees for their exhibitors.

Other places to look for mailing lists include the Standard Rate and Data Service directory, published by VNU, or the Directory of Associations (i.e., Gale Research), both of which are found in many large libraries and list publications and associations, respectively, that sell their lists. In addition, Karen Duncan of Union Park Appearance Care Center in Wilmington, Delaware, had good luck drumming up new business using a real estate broker customer list that she obtained through her county government.

Lists are usually rented to you for one-time use at a flat rate of anywhere from $40 to $100 per 1,000 names. You can usually get the lists on either pressure-sensitive labels or disk. Because the minimum number of names you can buy is usually 1,000, you can do your own random sampling by removing every nth label (as in 4th or 10th) or delete records from the disk until you get the number you want.

Before renting a mailing list, ask for references and see if other people had good experiences from a list rental company. The reality is that lists are compiled in all sorts of manners and some contain dated names and information that includes people who are no longer living at such addresses or have such phone numbers. Others names may have been obtained illegally. Get some feedback and make sure others have had positive experiences using the mailing lists. No list will be 100 percent accurate, but you do want the vast majority of your mailings to go to currently viable addresses.

Surveys don't have to be fancy, but they do have to be neat, spelled correctly, and professional looking. To save money, you can design the survey on your home computer (make sure it's clean and uncluttered). Then stop by a shop like Staples and have it photocopied on quality paper. You'll pay only about 8 cents per copy. (Office Max, for example, has a great online printing service—you tell them how many copies, what color paper you want, etc., then you attach your document, and the job will be ready for you at the store you designate.)

Secondary Research

If you're on a tight budget, you may have to rely more heavily on secondary research. Thanks to the internet, you may not have to spend a dime of your startup money on research. You just need to know where to look to find information that will help you make intelligent marketing assumptions. So start with local utility companies, which may even share their demographic info free of charge; local economic development organizations; your local municipality (city, county, parish, etc.), which keep census tracts on file that include information about population density and distribution; and your friendly Uncle Sam, who collects data on just about anything you can think of. The only problem with federal data is that it's not always fresh—it's often a year or two old since the wheels of the government grind slowly—but it still may be useful (and since it's usually free, the price is right). Sources that might be of help include the granddaddy of information gathering, the U.S. Census Bureau (www.census.gov), as well as the SBA (www.sba.gov). Most towns, communities, and municipalities have their own websites. Check these for local statistical information.

Once you start looking, you'll find that everyone has statistics they'll share. Not the least of these are your local library, chamber of commerce, trade publications (like Modern Car Care), and industry associations. There isn't a detailing trade association, but you can try one of the carwash organizations in the Appendix (regional ones are typically more likely to be helpful than the national ones). Finally, the Yellow Pages can be a useful source. The "Auto Detailing" listings can help you determine at a glance just how many legitimate detailers are already operating in your area and where they're located.

Customers and Competition

All the research in the world (primary or secondary) is worthless unless you utilize it properly. Using computer software, which could be an Excel spreadsheet or even just some sheets of paper, group your data into categories that will prove helpful to you. Don't be overly general or use only stereotypes. Get a feel for the actual data, not what

Market Research Questionnaire Postcard

—— Front of Postcard ——

From:

_____

_____

_____

↑ **Important!** Be sure to fill this out.

BUSINESS REPLY MAIL
FIRST-CLASS MAIL   PERMIT NO. 5555   CHICAGO, IL

POSTAGE WILL BE PAID BY ADDRESSEE

ATTN: **Daniel Wayne**
Great Lakes Automotive Detailing
5555 Jefferson Ave.
St. Clair Shores, MI 48051

- -

Fold Here

The automotive reconditioning and restoration experts

Tape Together Here

NO POSTAGE
NECESSARY
IF MAILED
IN THE
UNITED STATES

▲

Market Research Questionnaire Postcard, continued

Back of Postcard

Please answer the following questions and return this postage-paid card for a chance to win a complete detailing package valued at $185.

1. What kind of vehicle do you drive?
   _____
   _____

2. Have you ever had it professionally detailed?
   ❑ Yes
   ❑ No

   If no, skip to question 6.
   If yes, how often do you have it detailed?
   ❑ Weekly
   ❑ Monthly
   ❑ Other (specify)_____
   _____

3. How much do you pay for interior/ exterior detailing? _____
   _____

4. Would you prefer mobile detailing to dropping your vehicle off at a detailing shop?
   ❑ Yes
   ❑ No

5. Which detailing service is most important to you?
   ❑ Hand wash and vacuum
   ❑ Hand wax
   ❑ Upholstery cleaning
   ❑ Carpet dyeing
   ❑ Odor removal
   ❑ Windshield repair
   ❑ Paintless dent repair
   ❑ Other (specify) _____

6. What is the most you'd spend for a complete detail?
   ❑ $125 ❑ $150
   ❑ more than $150

7. Which of the following are important to you when it comes to using a detailing shop? (Check all that apply.)
   ❑ Price
   ❑ Extended business hours
   ❑ Detailers' training
   ❑ Ability to drop off without an appointment
   ❑ Quick service time
   ❑ Wide selection of retail products

8. What is your age?
   ❑ 18–29   ❑ 30–45
   ❑ 46–60   ❑ 61 and up

9. What is your household income?
   ❑ Under $25,000
   ❑ $25,000–$40,000
   ❑ $40,001–$55,000
   ❑ $55,001–$70,000
   ❑ $70,001 and up

10. What is your profession?
    _____
    _____

11. Please provide your e-mail address to receive information about detailing specials:
    _____
    _____

Market Research Letter

July 19, 2007

Mr. Greg Jakub
5555 Allard
Grosse Pointe Woods, Michigan 48236

Dear Mr. Jakub:

Please accept as our gift the enclosed $10 gift certificate toward any service valued at $100 or more at the new Great Lakes Automotive Detailing, opening in St. Clair Shores on September 1.

At Great Lakes, we specialize in providing professional interior and exterior detailing for everything from luxury vehicles to family sedans. In addition to hand washing and waxing your vehicle, we'll make the interior look like new. We also offer engine cleaning, paintless dent repair, and odor removal, all of which can restore your vehicle to showroom condition.

We hope you'll take a moment to fill out the brief questionnaire we've enclosed so we can determine how we can serve you best. If you'll return the enclosed postage-paid card with your responses, your name will be entered in a drawing for a complete detailing package valued at $185.

We look forward to serving you soon.

Very truly yours,

Daniel Wayne

Daniel Wayne
Owner
Great Lakes Automotive Detailing

5555 Jefferson Ave. · St. Clair Shores, Michigan 48051 · (555) 555-0000
www.greatlakesdetailing.com · info@greatlakesdetailing.com

▲

Guerrilla Marketing

Dave Echnoz of 14/69 Carwash Supercenter in Fort Wayne, Indiana, developed a surefire way to pick up new dealership business—he asked for it. Once a week, he'd drive to all the car lots in the area and note which new and used cars needed detailing. Then on Monday morning, he'd call the dealership managers and make a specific pitch, like "There's a blue Ford on your lot that needs work. I can come by and pick it up, and have it ready for you today."

This approach worked like a charm for both new and used vehicles. "Dealerships like that aggressive nature," Echnoz says. "And when I'd get there with the car, I'd offer to take another one back with me."

you'd expect to see, or what you'd like to see. Your goal should be to draw up a profile of your ideal customer, or customers. From this, you can branch out a little, some older, some younger, etc.

Finally, data about your competition is significant. Look at primary competition (detailers with shops like the one you will be opening) and secondary competition, such as mobile detailers or other locations that do some detailing. This will help you answer the following key questions;

- Is the market over saturated or underserved?
- Can I be competitive in price and still make a profit?
- What can I do to gain a competitive edge?
- Are there businesses with which I can align (that are not already working with the competition) such as used car dealers, limousine rental companies, or car washes?

Map Your Course

So now you're on track to understanding your market. Next up is the process of understanding yourself and your purpose, both of which help your business head in the right direction—right toward profitability and success. An effective way to do this is by writing a mission statement just like the big corporations do.

Even if you've never been to business school, you probably already have an insight into the process of a strong mission statement. Remember the scene in the 1996 movie "Jerry Maguire," when the title character, played by Tom Cruise, writes a description of everything that's wrong about being a sports agent and gives "a suggestion for the future of our company"? Basically, what he wrote was a mission statement, although at 30 pages it was more like a mission novel.

Your mission statement should briefly describe your company's purpose and goals. A one- or two-sentence mission statement should cover what your company does, who the customers should be, and why you do what you do.

A simple mission statement for a detailer might say this: "Great Lakes Auto Detailing will cater to the car-care needs of busy professionals and classic car owners by providing complete detailing and paintless dent repair services from a centrally located facility. The goal is to have an active client base of 100 people in the first six months."

Here's another possible approach: "Great Lakes Auto Detailing is a full-service car-care business that uses professional-grade equipment as a way to exceed the quality of service provided by its three nearest competitors. This level of professionalism, plus my skill and attention to detail, will lead to first-year sales of $60,000."

Here are a couple of actual mission statements provided by detailers that we spoke to:

"To provide exceptional value and customer care to the motoring public by maintaining the beauty of their vehicles."
—Detail in Progress, San Diego

"The purpose of Gem Auto is to provide the general public with a service by which they can restore, enhance, and/or maintain the appearance of the interior and exterior of their vehicle. We remain convenient to everyone in our market area and offer services that stay within the affordability of any car owner."
—Gem Auto Appearance Center, Waldorf, Maryland

As you can see, mission statements can be of varying lengths (the classic is Pepsi's two-word mission statement: "Beat Coke"), but the length isn't as important as what it means to you. For this reason, it's a good idea to review your mission statement regularly to make sure your business is moving toward achieving its goals.

On page 36 you'll find a worksheet that you can use to help you with the process of creating the right mission statement of our business. Don't worry if you don't get it right (or perfect) the first time. Business owners rewrite and edit their mission statements again and again until they have the few words that sound best and make the most accurate statement about the business.

▲

Mission Statement Worksheet

Here's your chance to try your hand at writing your own mission statement. Start out by answering the following questions:

1. Why do you want to start an auto detailing business? _____
   _____
   _____
   _____

2. What skills do you bring to the business? (Include education and detailing skills.) _____
   _____
   _____

3. What is your vision for success? Where do you think you'll be in one, two, and five years? _____
   _____
   _____

4. Which services do you want to offer? _____
   _____
   _____

5. Which customers do you want to service? (Be specific—e.g., general public, auto dealerships, both.) _____
   _____
   _____

Using this information, write your mission statement here:

Mission Statement For
(your business name)

_____
_____
_____
_____
_____
_____
_____

Throttling Up
for Success

By now you should have a good idea whether there are enough gearheads, auto enthusiasts, and car collectors in your target market to keep your business revved up. But before you can fire up the extractor and get down to business, you need to build your own reliable business chassis from the ground up. That means addressing the standard equipment

▲

Startup Checklist

Here is a list of things you need to do before launching your business:

❑ Select a business name and apply for a dba.

❑ Select a business structure under which you choose to operate (and consult with an attorney for advice).

❑ Apply for a federal employer identification number (if you're forming a corporation, partnership or taking on employees).

❑ Check local zoning regulations for restrictions on homebased businesses, if applicable, or on where you can open a detailing business.

❑ Apply to your municipality for a business license. File any other necessary forms as mandated by your local or state government.

❑ Write a business plan.

❑ Write a marketing plan.

❑ Consult with an accountant regarding financial and tax considerations for establishing and operating a business.

that comes along with the joy of owning your own business: namely, legalities like picking the appropriate business form, selecting a name, and insuring the whole operation against liability and loss.

Business Structure

Among the very first things you should do is to select the legal business form under which you wish to operate. This is important for two reasons. First, since the IRS is going to be very interested in anything you do that makes money, you'll want to pick the type of business that has the best tax advantages for your particular situation. Second, each type of legal structure has certain benefits and disadvantages when it comes to owner liability. You need to choose carefully to protect yourself and your business.

In general, businesses operate as one of four basic legal entities: sole proprietorship, partnership, corporation, or limited liability company (LLC).

Sole Proprietorship

Out of the four common legal forms, the sole proprietorship is the easiest to form. In fact, all you have to do is select a business name, file some simple paperwork at the county or state level to establish a fictitious business name of your choice, obtain a business license in the municipality in which you'll operate, and open a business checking account in the business's new name. In general, you don't have to establish credit in the name of your business; rather, you can whip out your personal plastic to charge business purchases like office equipment or professional detailing products. This can vary by supplier, however. Check with the companies you do business with to determine whether it's necessary to establish a business account.

As a sole proprietor, you'll get tax benefits like business expense deductions even though you don't have to file a separate business tax return. Instead, business income and expenses are reported on Schedule C of your personal IRS Form 1040 tax return, and your profits are taxed as ordinary income. You will, however, pay an extra self-employment tax, which essentially is the other half of the Social Security tax that you have to pay because you're the employer of record.

Smart Tip

Tip...

If you operate your business under your own name, you can use your Social Security number as your federal ID. But if you choose another name, or you form a partnership or corporation, you must have a federal employment identification number. To apply for one, file form SS-4 (available at any IRS office or at www.irs.ustreas.gov).

As the sole owner, you reap all the profits from the business (minus Uncle Sam's generous portion, of course), you manage the business the way you want, and you're completely responsible for its actions. Therein lies the problem with sole proprietorships. As sole owner, you are also personally liable for any losses, bankruptcy claims, or legal actions (like liability suits) that may be brought against your business. Any, or

Beware!

If you're planning to sell detailing products, you need a seller's permit, which enables you to buy products for resale without paying sales tax. The permit may be free of charge, but you may have to post a security deposit. Check with your state's board of equalization or department of revenue to find out the requirements. You will also, typically, have to collect sales tax on your products when selling to customers in conjunction with your state's sales tax laws.

all, of these situations can quickly wipe out not only your business assets but also your personal assets, including savings accounts, stocks and bonds, vehicles, and even your house. That's a scary thought, particularly given the litigious society in which we are living today. As a result, good liability coverage is a must in this business, no matter whether you're detailing 15-year-old Yugos or Rolls-Royces. You'll find a discussion of insurance options in Chapter 5.

Another disadvantage of sole proprietorships is that you're liable for employees who make mistakes while working for you. There's insurance available to manage this liability (which we'll talk about later), but it could end up being insufficient to cover claims. Then your personal property would again be at risk.

Finally, sole proprietors sometimes find it difficult to obtain financing for their fledgling venture. As you'll see later in the book, you can establish a new detailing business with a fairly low capital outlay, but if your business requirements exceed your bank account and/or your credit line, you may find that commercial lenders will be reluctant to fill your coffers with much-needed cash. Those that are willing to ante up are likely to insist on collateral, which again puts your personal assets at risk.

Partnership

Although many detailers start out in the business as independent operators, you might have a good buddy who would make a good business partner. So a partnership might be the way to go. If you're so inclined, you could also form a partnership with your spouse even if he/she isn't actively involved in the business. That way, if something happens to you, your spouse would take possession of the business. Compare that setup to a sole proprietorship, which is dissolved when the owner dies or declares bankruptcy, and you can see the wisdom of at least considering a partnership with your better half.

There are two types of partnerships—general and limited. In a general partnership, each partner participates in the day-to-day operation of the business, from servicing customers to wrestling with balance sheets. In a limited partnership, a general partner manages the business while the limited partner supplies working capital but does not actively participate in daily operations. Unless you have a rich relative or wealthy friends in really high places, you're probably more likely to form a general partnership.

Like sole proprietorships, partnerships are easy to establish. All you need is a verbal or written agreement between the partners, although a written partnership is definitely recommended. You'll also need to establish a business checking account on which both (or all) partners can draw.

Business profits are divvied up among the partners based on the percentage of the business each owns; these profits are then taxed as personal income on each person's individual tax return. You'll also have to file a few federal forms related to the partnership, which are discussed in *IRS Publication 541, Partnerships.* You can pick up a copy of the guide at your local IRS office, or you can download it for free from the IRS website (www.irs.gov).

As you might expect, one major downside of a partnership is personal liability. Each partner is liable for the other's actions (like when your partner accidentally rolls a client's custom SUV after swerving to avoid an overturned kielbasa truck on the interstate). Each partner also assumes unlimited liability in the event the business is sued, which means that both personal and business assets would be at risk.

Because each partner is responsible for the actions of the other, a written agreement between partners is strongly recommended, even if you've known your prospective business partner for years or are related to him/her. This includes spouses, since a partnership is dissolved upon the death or bankruptcy of one of the partners unless the partnership agreement stipulates otherwise. Have an attorney with small-business experience draw up an agreement that spells out all the terms of the partnership, including responsibilities, rights, and percentage of business ownership. This protects the remaining partner and his/her interests if one of you decides to leave the business or you have to dissolve the partnership for any reason (divorce, bankruptcy, relocation, etc.). You'll find information about hiring an attorney in Chapter 5.

The other drawback of a partnership is how such an agreement can be dissolved, if necessary. Many friends and relatives have ended up in court battles because they wanted to part ways and did not have an exit plan built into the partnership agreement. This is very important in order to save you potential legal battles. Additionally, such a partnership agreement should iron out as many potential battles as you see forthcoming.

Corporation

If limiting your liability is high on your priority list (as it would be if you're planning to detail high-end or collectible vehicles), then establishing a corporation is a smart move. A corporation is considered to be an entity completely separate from the business owner and, as such, is responsible for its own debts and actions, including liability. Of course, forming a corporation means filing numerous forms and following various requirements as stipulated by the state in which you incorporate, which typically incorporates minutes of board meetings.

The most common type of corporation is the C corporation, which offers limited liability protection, tax benefits for the health and life insurance premiums you pay, and the ability to transfer ownership if you decide to change careers or retire to Aruba. But these benefits don't come cheap; business profits are taxed twice, first at the corporate tax rate, then again at the personal tax rate because the owner and all employees are considered employees of the corporation. That can take a big bite out of profits.

An S corporation may be a more attractive choice for a detailer. With an S corporation, only the owner pays personal taxes on the profits—the corporation isn't liable. This preserves

> **Tip...**
>
> **Smart Tip**
> An S corporation or LLC may be the best choice for a detailing shop with one to five employees, while a C corporation may be more advantageous for a larger shop, according to detailing industry expert R. L. "Bud" Abraham. Consult your attorney and accountant for help choosing which one suits your situation best.

more of the profits, but there are fewer tax deductions and more restrictions. For instance, you'll be required to file articles of incorporation, elect officers (relatives are A-OK), and hold an annual meeting. The good news is that an informal meeting with a written agenda held in a service bay amidst your buffers and clay bars will fulfill the annual meeting requirement. The other good news is that you'll probably find it easier to obtain any startup financing you need if you're incorporated, although the lending institution may still require you to offer personal assets (a car, investments, or your home) as collateral.

When you're ready to establish your corporation, you should consult with an attorney to help you make the right decision on which type to choose. He or she also can handle the incorporation. However, the incorporation process isn't very complicated, so if you're adventurous you can do the job yourself. A do-it-yourself incorporation costs about $50 to $300 vs. $400 to $1,000 when handled by an attorney.

Limited Liability Company

Another common type of business entity is the limited liability company, or LLC. This type of business format has gained popularity recently because it combines the tax structure of a partnership yet protects the business owner from personal liability the way a corporation does. It's often compared to the S corporation because of its tax advantages. Your attorney can help you determine whether an LLC is the right legal form for your detailing business.

The Name of the Game

Now that you've decided on a business structure, you'll need to select a business name that suggests high performance and attention to detail while evoking the type of service you offer.

Here are the names of some detailing shops currently operating around the country:

- Angel's Detail Shop
- Attention to Detail
- Bear Essentials Auto Salon
- Big Poppa's Auto Detailing
- Canuck Cleaning Service
- Chief's Squeaky Clean
- Jolly Wolly Detail Shop
- Littleton Auto Detailing
- Khan Komplete Kar Kare Service
- Perfect Auto Finish

- Perfection Plus Auto Detailing
- Pristine Auto Detail
- Rick's Custom Detail Shop Inc.
- Sparkling Image Detail & Custom Work

Which ones appeal to you? Probably the ones that are clever or catchy. A lot of auto detailers choose creative names that channel auto themes (like Speedway Auto Laundry), possibly because ordinary names are too boring for America's car-crazy society. Or maybe it's because a lofty name pumps up the image of the business the same way a V-12 turbocharges a hot car.

Be that as it may, when you're choosing a name, stay away from ones that are too over-the-top, like "Race to the Finish Auto Detailing" or "The Suds Stud." If it's too cute, it won't work well in this industry, because it tends to make you seem less professional. That, in turn, can undermine the confidence your clientele will have in you to get the job done well. Need some help selecting the perfect name? You'll find a worksheet you can use to brainstorm ideas on page 44. You can also check the Yellow Pages (both the real and the virtual versions) for idea starters.

By the way, even though clever names tend to be more memorable, that doesn't mean you shouldn't name your detailing business after yourself. A simple, business-like name consisting of your name and a business description (like Mitch's Auto Detailing) can make the business seem more credible and reliable. It's also beneficial because many people like dealing with the owner of the company. So unless you have a name people will find difficult to pronounce, like "Bill Przewodniczki," feel free to name your offspring after its mom or dad.

If you do decide to use your own name, you should open a business checking account immediately to make it easier to distinguish between business deposits/ expenditures and personal transactions. The wisdom of doing so will become very clear to you at 11:59 P.M. on April 15, as you struggle to separate the legitimate business transactions from the receipts for day care, groceries, and so on.

Once you've selected the name, take it out for a test spin before you invest in any promotional materials or a Yellow Pages ad. Have a friend call you a few times so you can answer the phone using the new name. It should be easy to say (just imagine saying, "Phil Vandevere's Speedy Auto Detailing Shop" a few dozen times a day). Names heavy on alliteration ("Sunshine State Detail Shop") and those with words that are hard to distinguish over the phone ("Buck's Auto Express") also should be avoided.

Staking a Name Claim

Once you've settled on the perfect moniker for your business, it has to be registered— usually at the county, borough, or parish level—to ensure its uniqueness. This simple

Business Name Worksheet

Would you prefer not to use your own name in your business name but you're having some trouble selecting the perfect moniker? Try using this worksheet as an idea starter.

First, list the top three things that come to mind when you think of the word "detailing" (such as adjectives like "perfect" or "manicured," or nouns like "carpet"). Be creative!

1. _____
2. _____
3. _____

Next, list the top three things that come to mind when you think of the word "automobile."

1. _____
2. _____
3. _____

List three unique landmarks or other geographical references relevant to your city, state, or regional area that characterize the marketplace where you're located (like the St. Louis Arch or Times Square).

1. _____
2. _____
3. _____

Now, try combining elements from these three sections in different ways.

1. _____
2. _____
3. _____

Once you've come up with something you like, try putting it to the test:

❏ Say it aloud several times to make sure it's easily understood, both in person and over the phone. (Remember the name "The Suds Stud?" Besides being a terrible name, the "s" sounds make it difficult to pronounce, let alone understand on the phone.)

❏ Thumb through your local Yellow Pages directory to make sure someone else isn't already using the name you've chosen.

❏ Check with your county seat or other official registrar to make sure the name is available (since someone may have already claimed the name but may not be using it yet).

If your name passes these tests, then you're ready to officially register it.

process is necessary because, in essence, you're establishing a fictitious identity (even if you use your own name in the company name) and only one company at a time can have the same name in your market area.

To register a new business name, you must file an "assumed name" or dba ("doing business as") statement. It will cost you $10 to $50 to register the name, which gives you the privilege of using the name for a limited period of time, usually three to five years. When the time expires, you simply renew the dba by paying another fee. If you keep anteing up, you basically can have the name forever. But before you get permission to operate under your dba, a search is done by the government entity that accepts your application to make sure the name isn't already in use. You might be able to do the search yourself by logging on to the local government entity's website and searching the online business registry. If you happen to choose a name that's already being used, you'll have to pick something else, so it's a good idea to come up with a couple of names when you do your initial brainstorming. In this age of web marketing and using websites for advertising, you will also want to consider whether there is a website with the domain name currently in use. Here too, you can do your own simple web search for the domain name.

That's My Name!

In addition to making sure no one else is using the business name you've selected at the local level, you should also do a wider search to make sure you're not infringing on someone else's name. Companies and even individuals get pretty upset about that.

There are many places you can search on the internet for name conflicts. Among them are:

- ○ Your state's secretary of state or Department of Motor Vehicles office, which may have a searchable database of names against which you can compare your name
- ○ The U.S. Patent and Trademark Office website (www.uspto.gov)
- ○ Business directories such as InfoSpace.com, InfoUSA.com, or Bigyellow.com
- ○ Popular internet portals like Yahoo! and Google (plug in your name and see what comes up)
- ○ Network Solutions (www.networksolutions.com) and www.register.com, both of which can tell you whether your name is already being used as a domain name

Vroooooooom with a View

At this point in the business development process, it's likely you've already made some decisions about whether you're going to establish a mobile business, or intend to work out of your garage at home or in a commercial facility. If you're planning to detail cars in your driveway, you should be aware that there could be local ordinances that restrict or ban businesses from operating in residential areas. The idea, of course, is to protect homeowners from excessive traffic and noise, both of which you might generate with a homebased detailing business. For instance, the equipment you'll be using—vacuums, extractors, and buffers—tend to be loud, especially if it's running all day long. If you offer pickup and delivery service, you could have several customers' vehicles parked at your home, which could be seen as a traffic hazard. And if you're a mobile detailer, you may have to park your rig in the street when you're not on the road detailing cars, where it could be viewed as an unsightly obstacle to smooth traffic flow. It's not likely you'll be allowed to erect a sign on your front lawn to drum up business.

So, to avoid a lot of bureaucratic hassle, be sure to check with your local government office early in the process of establishing the business to see if homebased businesses are allowed. You may find you'll need special permits to operate as well as a business license. Such a license is usually quite inexpensive and is renewable annually. If, by chance, you're turned down for a license because of zoning restrictions, you can apply for (and possibly receive) a variance from the municipal planning commission. Plan to attend the commission's next meeting to show that your business won't disrupt the neighborhood. Having an extra-long driveway where you can park cars or installing sound deadening panels on the walls of your garage are measures you can take to help convince the municipal denizens that you'll be a good neighbor.

Business Details

Now that you've got all that corporate and legal stuff out of the way, you're well on your way to getting your business up and running. What you need now is a road map to guide your steps as you build a viable and profitable auto enterprise. That road map is your business plan. Such a plan outlines your plans, goals, and strategies for making your business successful and, as such, should be referred to often. It keeps you on track by helping you manage your business in the most professional way possible. But it also should be adaptable so it can change to meet current challenges and opportunities in your market.

In addition to keeping your ride on the road, there's another good reason to have a carefully developed business plan. Banks and other financial institutions expect you to have one when you apply for financing for your business. Most of the time they won't even consider a credit application from a business that doesn't have a comprehensive business plan; your business plan demonstrates that you're serious about your detailing business and have developed a viable plan to make it successful.

Even if you self-finance your business, you should have a detailed business plan. You need not consider yourself a writer to be able to draw up your own viable plan.

Business Plan Basics

There are books, articles, websites, and software packages designed to guide you through the steps of putting together a business plan,

Smart Tip

Tip...

The Small Business Association (SBA) has a wealth of free publications that can be helpful to small businesses. Two to try: Publication MP 21, Developing a Strategic Business Plan, and Publication MP 31, Handbook for Small Business. They're both available at local SBA offices or by visiting www.sba.gov/library.

complete with templates to follow so you need not reinvent the wheel. The business plan basics that follow are designed to start you thinking about possibilities.

Business plans are typically broken up into several key sections in an effort to outline and explain each area of the business. It is a means of putting together all the pieces of what is a large puzzle—the pieces that start up a business.

Included in a typical business plan, will be the following:

1. **Executive Summary.** This is a short, broad, yet enticing, summary of the business. What is the business all about and why are you excited about it? Although it usually appears first, this part is often written last, after you've put all the pieces in place.

2. **Products and/or Services.** Here you can include specific items that you will sell or services you will offer. Include products and services you expect to offer down the road. Explain their value and why they will be sought out by your customers.

3. **Industry Analysis.** Here you will paint a picture of the overall auto detailing industry in which your business will be a player. From your research, talk about the "big picture." By learning about, and writing a short report on the auto detailing industry, you personally will learn more about the industry in which you are about to embark.

4. **Competitive Analysis.** This is a biggie. Do your research carefully and know who you are up against. Be realistic and list the strengths and weaknesses of the most direct competitors. Don't trash the competition, it is not professional. Then, see if you can provide something—a new service, better customer service, something that your competitors do not provide. This can be your competitive edge.

5. **Marketing and Sales.** Now that you have plenty of details regarding what you will be selling, you need to explain how you will let the world know that you

are in business. In this section, you discuss your plans for marketing and promoting your business as well as how you will sell your services. This is where you define your plan of attack. If you are seeking funding, this is a very important section.

6. **Management.** Another important section is management, where you will let readers know who is running the business. Potential financial backers will be particularly interested in this information, since they want to know to whom they are lending their money. Include all of the key people involved in making this business happen. If this is a solo venture, use a bio that features applicable experiences in your career, or personal life, that applies to this venture, such as attending car shows and your years spent detailing the cars of friends and neighbors when you were just getting interested in the business.

7. **Operations.** From whether you are going mobile or setting up your own shop to how many cars you anticipate detailing in a week, or even in a day, this is where you can walk your readers through a day in the life of your detailing business. Besides the actual work on cars and trucks, or vans, remember to include your plan for all of the "office" responsibilities, such as taking mornings to order supplies and late afternoons for a full clean up. Think about how the operation will work start to finish.

8. **Financial Pages, or Forms.** The goal here is, with help from your accountant or financial planner, to make realistic projections based on researching similar businesses. Here is where you show the math problems we demonstrated earlier and then project on a years worth of profits and/or losses. Then show how long it will take to start showing a profit. Also include a cash and balance sheet for a year to show a cash flow. Hint: Be conservative in your financial estimates.

9. **Financial Requirement.** Very important, if you are seeking funding, this is where you include the amount of financing needed, based on the previous sections, to reach your goals. Again, be realistic, research costs carefully, and also indicate how much money you anticipate putting into the business venture yourself. Hint: You stand a much greater chance of getting investors interested, or bankers to approve a loan, if you have invested your own money into a business.

> **Stat Fact**
> A thoroughly researched business plan is about 25 pages long and can take 300 hours to prepare (which includes doing the research, compiling financial information, conducting surveys, and writing). But detailer Tom Schurmann reports the effort is worth it—after he wowed the bank with his 40-page business plan, he got the financing he needed in one day.

Add to this supporting documentation, which will include various financial reports and you will have a business plan. Do not try to dazzle prospective readers with hype, but provide the real story of the business so that it is clear on paper how it will operate and when you anticipate making money.

Of course, this is just a very basic outline. Before you sit down and start writing, you will need to do research and look at other business plans in books or online to see the phrasing and style of such a business plan. If nothing else, thinking about each aspect of the plan will force you to start thinking about all of the many details that go into starting up a business. That's when it gets exciting, and a little scary, as you see all of the pieces come together.

If you need assistance, contact your local Small Business Development Center (found in the federal section of the Yellow Pages under the SBA or by logging on to www.sba.gov/sbdc) or check your local bookstore or library for one of the many books or software packages available that make writing a business plan a manageable task.

The final task is editing and proofreading your plan very carefully before showing it to anyone. Neatness and a good presentation count if you are looking for funding.

Under the Hood:
Choosing a Professional Pit Crew

So far we've talked about the structure of your detailing business and the mechanics of establishing it properly. Now it's time to consider the people you'll need on your team to keep the business humming along. Those professionals include an attorney, an accountant, and an insurance agent.

Now you might be thinking, "Hey, I'm just a little guy trying to make a living. I haven't even bought any Armor All yet, and you're telling me I need a bunch of high-priced consultants?"

Well, yes. No matter how large your detailing operation is—from a one-person mobile operation to a business with employees and a fixed location—you need experienced professionals who can help you avoid common startup blunders and free you from the mundane aspects of running the business, like preparing your corporate taxes and reading carefully through contracts, that you will likely have questions about anyway. You need to free up your time to spend on the activities you do best—like detailing cars, SUVs, and trucks. Having these pros on your management team will help make your business seem much more stable and solid. Additionally, it will be easier to attract the attention of bankers, suppliers, and others with which you will either do business or look to obtain financing.

A Powerful Ally

Trial attorney Henry G. Miller once said, "The legal system is often a mystery, and we, its priests, preside over rituals baffling to everyday citizens." That pretty much sums up why you need an attorney on your business team.

A trustworthy, competent business attorney is invaluable for sorting out the intricacies of the law, from negotiating leases and reading contracts to defending you against unfounded claims of detailing crimes committed on a vehicle. He/she also can help you with tax planning, lease and loan negotiations as well as reviewing contracts that you present to new clients. Even the one-person detailer should have an attorney on standby for those unexpected things that tend to pop up when you're in business for yourself.

Believe it or not, it's possible to find an attorney whose fee schedule fits into your budget. To keep costs down, avoid large law firms, which tend to service larger clients with big corporate bankrolls, and opt instead for a one- or two-person practice. Even in a small firm, rates typically start at around $100 per hour, but the denizens of those smaller practices are more likely to be willing to work within your humble budget and not run up numerous hours.

You'll probably find it most cost-effective to engage an attorney who charges a flat fee for routine work, such as writing letters or

Dollar Stretcher

A prepaid legal plan can be a great way to save money on attorney fees. You just pay a small annual fee to get services like telephone consultations, letter writing, and contract review provided by a qualified attorney. The plans also may provide legal representation at a reduced cost. You can find attorneys who provide such services in the phone directory under "Legal Service Plans."

Count on It

If you need an accountant but you don't have a lot of cash for the fees, consider using a public accountant rather than a CPA. Public accountants aren't state-licensed, so they generally charge less than CPAs. But they also can't represent you before the IRS if you're called in for an audit. CPAs, on the other hand, are college-educated and have to pass a rigorous state-administered certification examination. Most business experts recommend using only CPAs because their credentials are universally recognized and respected by bankers, investors, and others in the business world.

To keep tax preparation costs under control, look for an enrolled agent instead of an accountant. They're fully qualified to represent you before the IRS in case of an audit. Enrolled agents can be found in the Yellow Pages under "Accountants" or through the directory found on the National Association of Enrolled Agents' website at naea.org.

setting up a corporation, or one who offers a business startup package. Such packages usually include the initial consultation and all activities related to the incorporation process, including the filing of paperwork with your state and other corporate formalities. You can expect to pay around $900 for this service. Other common fee arrangements include paying an upfront retainer, out of which the attorney draws as work is completed, or paying via contingency, which means the attorney is paid a percentage of whatever is won in a lawsuit settlement.

To find an attorney who suits you, ask around. Other small-business owners are the best sources for recommendations as are organizations like the chamber of commerce or your local economic development group. Barring that, you can try an attorney referral service, which can be found in many counties around the country. Remember, you are better served by someone familiar with your type of business, or at least service businesses, rather than hiring your brother-in-law the divorce attorney.

Money Matters

The complexity of tax laws notwithstanding, having an accountant available to handle your money matters is a cost-saving strategy for any business. While you can hire a bookkeeper at a lower rate to come in and handle your weekly and monthly books, an accountant can oversee the big picture—the budget, necessary tax payments, and your financial needs. He or she can help you determine how much money you can afford to spend in specific areas and how much you will need to put aside for taxes. Should you be poor at keeping records and receipts, a bookkeeper can handle this for you and an accountant can make sure that such record keeping is in proper format, since Uncle Sam likes things done his way. If you elect to handle your own bookkeeping, you can utilize anything from a simple spreadsheet program like Microsoft Excel to a more complex bookkeeping software suite. Programs like QuickBooks also have a feature that allows you (or your accountant) to download financial records and other information entered into your worksheets directly to TurboTax business tax software, which is a great timesaver at tax time.

However, software does not replace a human being who can answer tax and money questions that are specific to your business, which will likely arise. For this reason, consider an accountant. A good accountant can provide guidance and advice.

Accountants are skilled at handling important tasks like creating profit and loss statements, making financial projections, forecasting cash flow, and setting up accounting systems—all of which are important to even the smallest business. In addition, an experienced accountant is invaluable for interpreting tax law, which is very complicated and changes frequently. (In fact, the IRS issues new tax rulings every few hours of every business day!)

For all this expertise, you can expect to pay an hourly rate that varies by type of practice, location, expertise, and education. Typically, you can expect to pay anywhere from $35 to $100 an hour depending on the level of experience of the accountant and that market in which your business resides.

Your attorney, banker, or other business owners in the detailing or carwash industry are good sources of referrals. Alternatively, the American Institute of Certified Public Accountants' branch in your state can refer you to a qualified CPA, or you can find a professional accountant at www.accountant-finder.com. It's preferable to select someone who has experience with small-business clients because they're more likely to be tuned in to your tax and financial situation.

Finding an accountant, like finding an attorney, can come via recommendations from friends or associations. You can always use the Yellow Pages or do a search online for accountants in your area.

Managing Risk

Anyone who's ever owned a vehicle knows the necessity of having good car insurance. In this country, even clunkers have to be insured, even if it's only to protect the other guy against the damage your decrepit battle cruiser might inflict in a collision.

The same theory applies to your new detailing business. You'll need coverage to protect yourself against a carload of what-ifs (hark back for a moment to what we said about liability in Chapter 4). To help you steer through the winding back roads of Insuranceville, you'll want to rely on the services of a professional insurance broker.

An insurance broker differs from an insurance agent because a broker represents may different insurance products from many different companies, while "regular" insurance agents are employed by a single company and sell only that company's products. Going with a broker is advantageous for two reasons. First, the broker won't be attached to any one company's products and will, therefore, be more objective and willing to shop around on your behalf. Second, by comparing many policies and levels of coverage against one another, a broker often can get you a good insurance policy at a rate you can afford.

To find a reputable business insurance broker, tap your business acquaintances or attorney for recommendations, or look in the "Business" subcategory of the "Insurance" listings in the phone directory for leads. It's best to select a broker who understands the concerns of small-business owners, especially those who need good liability insurance (a primary requirement for auto detailers like you). Ask to see a client list when you talk to a prospective broker to get a feel for the types of clients he/she services. In today's litigious society, you are always a target (as are all service providers) for a lawsuit based on someone's presumption that you did something wrong.

One of the most important decisions you'll make when buying business insurance is determining exactly how much coverage you'll need, based on how much risk you're willing and financially able to take. That means if you're going to specialize in high-end vehicles like sports cars or classic cars, you'll need a liability policy with higher coverage than if you detail the family sedans of the world.

Not surprisingly, many detailers don't approach their business insurance needs this way. Instead, they're more concerned with cutting corners to control costs, and, as a result, they're often underinsured—if they're insured at all. But the problem is that all it takes is one disaster—like having an inexperienced technician enthusiastically power-buff a classic car right down to the metal or hosting the first tornado to

> **Tip...**
>
> ## Smart Tip
>
> A commonsense approach to risk management can help you avoid accidents in the shop or on a mobile job. For instance, don't let employees do work they're not qualified to perform. Be sure to eliminate trip-and-fall hazards like piles of wet towels in the work area and ice in your parking lot, and make sure your ground fault interrupter outlets aren't overloaded. Also, remember signage that warns against potential hazards on the property and contracts that state clearly what you are and are not responsible for—to be written with help from the above-mentioned attorney and then read (and signed) by your clients.

roar through your community in half a century—and your entire business could be wiped out.

"There seems to be a certain amount of resistance to insurance, especially among smaller operators," says Prentice St. Clair, a San Diego detailing industry expert and mobile detailer, in an article in *Modern Car Care* magazine. "Part of this stems from the cost of insurance and part of it from lack of understanding of the type of insurance you need. But without insurance, you are exposing yourself, your business, and your family to the gamble that nothing bad will ever happen while you are operating your business. But regardless of how careful you are or how good your intentions are, it only takes one accident or frivolous lawsuit to destroy your business, with all its earning potential."

St. Clair admits that in the early days of his detailing business, he operated without insurance. "But knowing what I know now, I would never be without insurance, regardless of the cost," he says.

Types of Insurance

Although there is insurance available to cover just about any situation imaginable, from negligence to property damage to glass breakage, no small-business owner can afford to insure against everything that can go wrong (Murphy's Law notwithstanding). Rather, you just have to assume some of the risk, then buy sufficient insurance

Go for Broke(r)

If you're considering buying or leasing a building for a detailing shop, you should consider consulting a professional real estate broker. A broker can be invaluable for helping you find the perfect location—especially in a tight real estate market—because he/she will know which commercial locations are available that would suit your needs, how dynamic the area you're considering is in terms of growth potential, and how much space goes for in the target area. He/she also can act as an intermediary with the seller or landlord and then help with negotiations when you're ready to sign on the dotted line. If you use a broker, be sure to find out up front who pays the broker's fee. Sometimes the seller pays the fee; other times, the seller and the buyer split the fee. If you're footing the bill, you'll be expected to sign a contract agreeing to pay for services rendered. Don't rely solely on a broker. Have your attorney review all contracts and agreements.

▲

> ## Beware!
> To qualify for the self-employed health insurance deduction, the insurance plan must be established under your business name. The IRS says that the deduction may be allowed if you either paid the premiums yourself, or your partnership or S corporation paid them. The premium amounts also must be included in your gross income.

to offset the more significant risk that would force your company into bankruptcy or cause serious financial problems. Generally speaking, the types of insurance detailers usually need are commercial garage keeper's liability insurance, property insurance, and business interruption insurance. If you have employees, you also will need workers' compensation insurance.

Commercial Garagekeeper's Liability Insurance

This is the single most important type of coverage you will need for your detailing business. It covers damage to customers' vehicles, damage incurred if you're involved in an accident while driving a customer's vehicle, and injuries that happen at your place of business (including the injuries sustained by waiting customers who spill the cup of coffee they've been balancing dangerously on their knee). You may also need additional insurance, or a rider, if you send out mobile units from your fixed-site location.

Because you'll want your insurance to cover as much of the damage or lawsuit award as possible so your business will survive once a settlement has been made, it's imperative not to skimp on the amount of coverage you buy. Insurance industry experts recommend obtaining $1 million to $2 million of garage liability coverage, which shouldn't break your piggy bank because it's not priced on a dollar-for-dollar basis. Rather, it's usually based on the size of your business (including factors like square footage of your facility, assets, and number of employees) and the risks involved in day-to-day operations. Also, as with car insurance, the higher your deductible, the more affordable the insurance becomes.

Property Insurance

Also known as casualty insurance, property insurance protects both the building you're working out of (if you own it) and its contents. Among the incidents property insurance can protect against are major disasters (like acts of God), fire, vandalism, and so on, and the amount of coverage possible is determined by the value of the property. The insurance

> ## Smart Tip
> Commercial garage-keeper's liability insurance for a detailer who owns property should run about $2,000 per bay per year, according to auto reconditioning industry consultant Prentice St. Clair. A detailer with no employees should expect to pay about $1,200 a year.

company will send an appraiser out to place a value on the property before giving a quote.

Business Interruption Insurance

If the unthinkable happens and you're unable to operate due to a natural disaster or a fire, theft, or other insured loss, business interruption insurance will pay the cost of your normal business expenses while your business is shut down. In addition to covering lost income, it may cover expenses like equipment replacement, facility rental, and so on. The price is determined by how likely you are to face certain risks. For instance, the premium cost could be higher for a detailer because you'll be storing flammable materials (like sprays and polishes). It might also be higher if you are in a hurricane region or an area where flooding is more common. However, because it's possible for most detailers to work out of a temporary location while their facility is being repaired, interruption insurance costs may be somewhat lower than those of, say, a restaurant, which would be out of business if it was shuttered for some reason. Talk to your insurance broker about whether you should have this insurance and how much it would cost.

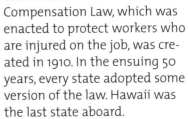

Fun Fact

The Uniform Workmen's Compensation Law, which was enacted to protect workers who are injured on the job, was created in 1910. In the ensuing 50 years, every state adopted some version of the law. Hawaii was the last state aboard.

Workers' Compensation Insurance

You are entitled to make some decisions when it comes to the other types of insurance discussed so far, but you don't have that luxury with workers' compensation insurance. Forty-nine states require employers to have workers' comp, which covers employees who have work-related injuries, diseases, and illnesses. (In Texas, the employers themselves are permitted to decide whether or not to provide workers' comp.) It's considered to be "no-fault" insurance, meaning the employer doesn't have to admit responsibility for any injury or illness, and the employee doesn't have to sue to get compensation.

Workers' comp insurance is such a complicated issue that it can't be handled in depth in this guide. But here are a few details you should know:

- Most states allow employers to purchase workers' comp through private insurance carriers. However, a few states require them to buy it through a state fund instead. For a list of those states, go to the U.S. Department of Labor's table at www.dol.gov/esa/regs/statutes/owcp/stwclaw/tables-pdf/table-1.pdf.

- The amount of coverage necessary and the percentage of salary paid to employees under workers' comp varies by state. Your insurance broker can fill you in on the details relating to your situation.

- Premiums also vary by state and are influenced by factors like payroll size, your industry (the more hazardous the industry, the higher the rate), and the severity of potential work injuries.
- The owner doesn't count as an employee under workers' comp law, so you're not covered by workers' comp. Because you're on your own, you should seriously consider buying business interruption insurance and paying the premiums on a personal health insurance policy.

Other Types of Insurance

As mentioned previously, you can get insurance to guard against just about any kind of risk. Other types to consider include:

- *Bonding insurance.* This protects you against loss incurred by employees who steal, either from you or your customers.
- *Disability insurance.* If you can't work due to injury or illness, this insurance will replace a percentage of your gross income. Self-employed people do not qualify for workers' comp insurance (because they're considered the employer of record, even if they don't actually have employees), so this is the way to go to make sure you have money coming in while you're recuperating.
- *Health insurance.* Beginning with the 2003 income tax filing year, the IRS allows a health-insurance-premiums deduction of 100 percent for self-employed people who report a net profit on Schedule C, C-EZ, or F. The cost of medical and dental insurance, as well as qualified long-term care insurance for yourself, your spouse, and your dependents all qualify for the deduction. (Here's where you need that accountant to make sure you take the deduction properly.) See IRS Publication 535, Business Expenses, for more information. By the way, offering health insurance to employees can be a good recruiting and retention tool, and those premiums are also deductible.
- *Life insurance.* In addition to protecting your family or significant other in case of your death, you may need a life insurance policy if you're planning to seek financing. It's not uncommon for banks to require business owners to have life insurance before they'll show them the money.

As you can see, an insurance broker really is invaluable for wading through the morass of

Tip...

Smart Tip

In the event of a loss, good insurance records are crucial. So be sure to keep receipts for every item purchased for the business; keep a written inventory of each item with the date of purchase, price, and current value; and either photograph or videotape the contents of each room. Then keep these documents in a safe place (like a safe deposit box), not in your shop.

insurance policies and options, then helping you decide which ones are right for you. To help you along, here's an insurance planning worksheet that you can use to compare policies and premiums.

Business Insurance Planning Worksheet		
Type	Required	Annual Cost
Commercial garagekeeper's liability		
Property		
Business interruption		
Workers' compensation	yes	
Bonding		
Disability		
Health		
Life		
Other		
Total Annual Cost		$

6

Detailing Tools
and Toys

Are you the type of person who gleefully wanders the aisles of an automotive superstore with eyes glazed over by the dizzying array of products to choose from? Do you pore over auto supply catalogs the same way kids memorize the toy section of the JC Penney Christmas catalog? Or do power tools—especially big, loud ones—send you into paroxysms of joy? Then you've definitely selected the right profession.

Detailers get to have all kinds of raucous fun with tools like gleaming stainless-steel power sprayers, rotary buffers that can polish a coconut to billiard-ball smoothness, and pressure washers that can repel an armadillo at ten paces. Then, add your choice of all the waxes, dressings, and polishes you could ever dream of to restore the showroom shine to even the oldest battle cruiser, and you have a profession to dye carpet for.

In this chapter, we've included typical prices for the higher priced items you may need to give you an idea of what you'll be spending, whether you're site-based or mobile. Equipment specific to mobile detailers is listed in its own section. To give you an idea of how typical expenses may add up, you'll find equipment and supplies cost breakdowns, and an equipment and supplies worksheet, on pages 80–82 that you can use to start jotting down your own business expenses.

Now, here's a rundown of all the equipment and supplies you may need to indulge your inner gearhead.

Power Tools and Accessories

Among the must-haves for either a fixed-site or mobile detailer are:

- *Air compressor.* This is for powering pneumatic tools. Make sure you buy an air compressor that has the power you need for your business ($400). Along with detailing, you can use an air compressor for other purposes such as blowing air out of dirty vents.

- *Random orbital polisher.* Go for pneumatic if you're going to install a compressed-air system; otherwise, electric is fine. In addition to buffing, this can be used to shampoo carpet and floor mats simply by using a brush attachment. They run about $150. Bonnets are used on this piece of equipment to remove cleaners, polish, wax, and other sealants. There are many to choose from at various prices, most under $10.

- *Variable-speed rotary buffer/polisher.* Available in pneumatic and electric versions, this tool creates friction and heat so surface irregularities can be corrected and a high shine can be achieved. Even those people who know little to nothing about detailing have heard of the buffer and polishers. Therefore, this is an important piece of equipment that you will use every day. Go top of the line if you can; they run roughly $225. The cut-

> **Smart Tip**
>
> Because you'll use your rotary buffer every day, consider buying a pneumatic model. They're not as heavy as the electric versions, so you won't get as tired after using it for a few hours. A variable-speed model that goes from 600 to 2,400 rpm is a versatile choice.

ting and finishing pads you need for this tool are available at various prices, generally around $10.

- *Pressure washer.* Experts recommend buying the highest-quality pressure washer you can afford because it will last longer and do a better job. Excellent for engine detailing, they start at about $1,000, but a really sweet model can be as much as $3,000. A good pressure washer should draw water from a standing tank, and most are equipped with soap injectors. Most are also easy to mount in trucks or vans. Those that include generators can run up to $4,500.

- *Stainless-steel tank sprayer.* This is for dispensing everything except acid. A three-gallon sprayer is the perfect size for a mobile operation and runs around $139. A five-gallon model is around $150. A tank cart for easily wheeling this type of sprayer to the work site runs roughly $125 to $175.

- *Vapor steam cleaner.* This is for power cleaning and deodorizing. Using vapor steamers is an environmental plus as it greatly reduces the amount of chemicals used while detailing. Commercial models run from $700 to $1,700.

- *Extractor.* A good extractor can clean carpeting and the upholstery, getting deep into fabric and extracting dirt. This pulls shampoo and rinse water out of carpeting and is preferred by professionals over wet-dry vacs because it has better suction power and thus prevents mildew in carpeting. Again, look for an extractor that will meet the needs of your business. A professional extractor will run about $1,500.

- *Wet-dry vacuum.* Detailers need a vacuum with a lot of power. You'll need at least a five-hp motor or it won't have enough power. Also, look for one with filters that are easy to find when you need to replace them. Think "powerful, rugged, and compact" when choosing a wet-dry vac. This runs about $350.

- *Ozone odor generator.* This very important device is for removing many odors, including

Smart Tip

Stock up on brushes, mitts, and plenty of towels. Detailers use a wide range of brushes including interior, exterior, tire, and engine brushes. In addition, you'll want numerous mitts and sponges so that you don't take the dirt from one job and deposit it on the next vehicle that rolls in. Also, stock up on cotton terrycloth towels. Buy these products in bulk for lower prices and look for high quality towels that won't start falling apart from a little elbow grease.

Beware!

Always buy the best tools you can afford and use them only in the way they're intended. The wrong cleaning tool can cause major damage, such as surface scratches or paint damage, which can take hours to repair.

tobacco smoke, spoiled food, mildew, pet deposits, and so on. They run from around $375 up to $1,000 and higher.

Additional tools that are particularly useful for detailers include a creeper for sliding under vehicles ($170); a temperature gauge for checking the temperature of paint ($80); a digital electronic or magnetic paint-thickness gauge, which helps you determine how much buffing the clearcoat can withstand ($500); and a photographer's loupe for getting a close-up view of flaws in the paint ($7). An interior dryer ($175) and a towel wringer ($120) are also great helpers for auto detailers.

Cleaning Products and Tools

Because prices can vary widely on cleaning products, we've provided you with a checklist (opposite page) of the numerous chemicals and other products you'll need. The Appendix has a list of suppliers you can check out when you're ready to buy.

It's also worth mentioning that the initial costs of the various add-on services can add hundreds of dollars to the cost of a basic detail. Yet these products have very low per-application materials costs. For instance, small vinyl and leather repairs cost less than $5, yet you can charge $25 to $75. Among these add-ons (and their costs to get started) are:

- Paintless dent repair (around $2,000 to $10,000 for a turnkey system with training)
- Paint touch-up (requires hands-on training to do well—$1,500 to $3,000)
- Vinyl and leather repair ($300 to $1,000)
- Carpet and fabric repair ($300 to $700)
- Carpet dyeing ($375)
- Gold-plating ($1,500 to $3,000)
- Windshield repair ($500 to $2,500)

Although this probably looks like a lot of stuff to buy, you'll find that the highest costs are for the power tools. Luckily, your equipment should last a long time if you buy high-quality tools. To really keep your costs down, check out online auction sites like eBay, where you can get some great bargains. For instance, a used Honda generator with low "mileage" that costs around $1,800 new was recently listed for $800. Everything else, from brushes to chemicals, is far less expensive, even if you do need a lot of items when you start out. But overall, you'll find

Bright Idea

Window tinting is another add-on service that can bring in big bucks for detailers. However, the skill is difficult to learn—curved windows are the hardest—and the job can take up to four hours to complete. A lot of detailers prefer to outsource this work and then mark up the service to make a few bucks.

Cleaning Products and Tools Checklist

Interior Cleaning Products

- ❑ Carpet and upholstery shampoo, protectant
- ❑ Upholstery shampoo, protectant
- ❑ Spot remover
- ❑ Tar, bug, and sap remover
- ❑ Deodorizer and disinfectant
- ❑ Ozone generator, odor remover, or fogger bombs (a less expensive alternative to an ozone generator)
- ❑ Cotton-tipped applicators (also used on the exterior to clean tight spots, like around taillight lenses)
- ❑ Vinyl cleaner, dressing, protectant, dyes
- ❑ Leather cleaner, conditioner, dyes
- ❑ Clear plastic cleaner

Exterior Cleaning Products

- ❑ Exterior shampoo
- ❑ Exterior vinyl and rubber dressing
- ❑ Detailing clay
- ❑ Buffing compounds in various grits
- ❑ Tar/grease remover
- ❑ Wax and silicone remover
- ❑ Presoak bug remover
- ❑ Decal remover
- ❑ Paint leveler (an acid rain/scratch remover)
- ❑ Carnauba and synthetic wax
- ❑ Vinyl and convertible top cleaner
- ❑ Microfine sandpaper grit (for color sanding, removing surface scratches)
- ❑ Glass cleaner
- ❑ Glass polish
- ❑ Aluminum polish
- ❑ Chrome polish
- ❑ Distilled white vinegar and ammonia
- ❑ Wheel cleaner, dressing, polish
- ❑ Rubber and black trim restorer
- ❑ Masking tape (to cover door, hood, trunk edges where paint is thin to prevent burning through it)
- ❑ Tire and wheel cleaner (If you buy it concentrated, you can then mix it for the strength you need.)
- ❑ Engine degreaser
- ❑ Oil: WD-40

Cleaning Tools

- ❑ Wheel/tire brush
- ❑ Spoke and slot brush
- ❑ Vent brush
- ❑ Carpet/fabric brush
- ❑ Sponges (natural)
- ❑ Spray and squeeze bottles
- ❑ Nylon bug/tar sponge
- ❑ Cotton- or foam-tipped applicators (for crevice cleaning)
- ❑ Engine detail brush
- ❑ Single-edge razor blades
- ❑ Chamois (natural chamois absorbs more water)
- ❑ Dry cleaning cloths (for removing film, dirt)
- ❑ Terrycloth towels (Detailing experts recommend having a different color for each application, including application and buffing of products, products with silicone, window washing, interior cleaning, etc.)
- ❑ Microfiber towels (now a favorite among detailers because they're softer and lint-free)
- ❑ Feather duster
- ❑ Squeegee
- ❑ Paper floor mats, seat covers
- ❑ Wool and foam pads
- ❑ Wax applicators
- ❑ Scrub brush
- ❑ Plastic bristle brush
- ❑ Wash mitts
- ❑ Steel wool package
- ❑ Window rags
- ❑ Long and short bristle paint brushes

Miscellaneous

- ❑ Creeper (for sliding easily under a vehicle)
- ❑ Towel wringer
- ❑ Interior dryer

Fast Track to Detail Success

Auto detailing and reconditioning systems help you get a fast start in the business by providing you with all the right equipment, support, and training as a package deal. Here are a few to consider if you're interested in this approach:

○ *Detail King.* This company offers auto detailing business startup packages that include equipment, supplies, training, and marketing support (www.detailking.com).

○ *Detail Plus Car Appearance Systems.* In addition to offering one of the most complete detailing and express detailing systems around, Detail Plus also has supplies, chemicals, and equipment (www.detailplus.com).

○ *National Detail Systems.* This company is known for auto detailing systems; mobile auto repair and reconditioning systems; as well as detailing products and equipment, training, and support; and has an online superstore for detailing supplies and car-care equipment (www.nationaldetail.com).

your supply costs will be pretty low from month to month, particularly when you consider just how much you can earn from them.

Now let's move on to some other detailing necessities.

Personal Protection Equipment

Anyone who works with power equipment for an extended period every day should consider wearing ear protection. It is known that shop tools operate at up to 90 decibels, according to Quiet Solution, a manufacturer of soundproofing products, whereas pneumatic drills operate at 110 decibels. OSHA says that since hearing damage can occur with even limited exposure to sound levels in the 85 to 90 dB range, hearing protection is recommended. You can pick up headset-style hearing protectors for around $15 a pair.

Safety glasses/goggles are also a good idea for protecting sensitive eyes from airborne chemicals and particles. They're a bargain at about $5 to $7 a pair.

Smart Tip

Sunblock or a strong sunscreen is a must for mobile detailers. Studies show that prolonged exposure to the sun (particularly during the hours of 10 A.M. to 3 P.M.) increases your risk of developing skin cancer. So everyone should wear a minimum 15 SPF sunscreen while working outdoors.

Uniforms and Hats

To increase the professionalism of your business, detailers should always wear clean, wrinkle-free uniform shirts while on the job. While a uniform company like Cintas can provide you with fresh uniforms, that can be expensive, especially for a one- or two-person detailing business. Instead, you can adopt embroidered polo shirts with collars as your company uniform. (Avoid T-shirts; they look too casual.) Personalized shirts (and baseball caps for mobile detailers) not only give you a neat, professional appearance, but are also a low-cost advertising tool. Plus here's an added bonus: The IRS considers shirts that have your company name and logo on them to be advertising and will allow you to deduct their cost. Embroidered polo shirts cost as little as $15 each, and hats run $12 to $17 each. You don't have to buy a lot of them to get this kind of pricing, either; some companies will sell you as few as six shirts at a time.

"Uniforms are a must," says Dave Echnoz of 14/69 Carwash Supercenter in Fort Wayne, Indiana. "The stereotypical detailer is a guy with a bandana, cut-offs, and a Budweiser in his hand who cusses all the time. Customers don't trust that kind of guy—they're going to worry that their Palm Pilot won't still be in the glove compartment after the work is done. So you have to look good on the job."

Echnoz also recommends paying just half of the uniform cost for full-time employees so they won't expect new shirts all the time. "And unless Nike is going to cut you a check to wear their hat, don't wear Nike. Get a personalized company hat," he adds.

Special Mobile Equipment

Although a mobile detailer will use many of the same tools and supplies listed earlier, there are a few other things you'll need to get into business. The very first thing is a

Going High Tech

Along with using the latest in vapor machines made in Italy, Perfect Auto Finish is utilizing "the CSI version of detailing," as Rennie Doyle, owner of the six facility detailing business, puts it. For people who often have their dogs in the cars, they can detect the source of the smells, such as urine, by using a black light with special glasses, much the way detective do in crime scene investigations. "Proteins show up with the black lights and we can then remove the problem," explains Doyle of the latest in high-tech detailing.

reliable vehicle in good repair—preferably a pickup truck with a covered bed—for hauling around your equipment. Vehicles that double as family transportation, including vans and SUVs, will also work, but of course you'll have to remove your detailing equipment before the family can pile in for a trip to the mall. Many mobile detailers prefer to have a vehicle dedicated to the business, and because payment and maintenance costs are fully deductible business expenses, it's usually not too hard—even for the detailer operating on a shoestring—to swing this expense. A reliable used truck or van should cost around $7,000 to $10,000, plus you'll need about $5,000 to equip it. If you prefer to go new, you can buy a low-end truck for around $15,000. For example, new 2008 Chevy Colorados start at just over $14,000 and run up to $24,000 with features, most of which you won't need. So estimate about $17,000.

Among the items you'll have to carry in your truck are a portable 125-gallon water tank (enough for a full day of washing), which will run about $279; a pressure washer ($900 to $2,500); a wet-dry vacuum ($355) or carpet extractor ($1,300); a variable-speed buffer ($200); and a generator to operate all your equipment (about $1,800). Another way to tote around all that equipment is with a detailing trailer that attaches to the back of your vehicle. For $5,500 to $10,000, you can get a trailer complete with a water tank, pressure washer, generator, air compressor, and toolbox—almost everything you'll need except supplies. You'll also need to carry a sufficient supply of detailing supplies, like brushes, and enough towels and chemicals to carry you through the day. Other useful items include portable florescent lighting for peering into those hard-to-see nooks and crannies under the hood ($195), and a portable space heater ($130) for when the temperature dips or you're forced to work after the sun goes down.

A portable pop-up tent is also a good idea for protecting yourself and your customers' cars from the elements, including sudden rain and excessive heat (which can

---

Smart Tip

Tip...

Although mobile detailing is a huge convenience for customers, it wastes time for the detailer because drive time is not billable. So whenever possible, schedule jobs in the same area for the same day, or arrange to be in a central location, such as an office complex, for an entire day. If you can work out a barter deal, whereby you detail someone's car in exchange for using his or her parking area throughout the day, you'll be all set.

However, you have to make sure:

a. Not to leave a mess

b. Not to disrupt his/her business

c. Not to cause traffic or parking problems.

In the right situation, if you plan it in advance, you can promote in advance that you will be doing detailing work for everyone in an office park or complex on a certain day and charge a group volume rate. Just make sure it's worth your while.

▲

affect the way certain products adhere to the paint). These tents are discussed in greater detail in Chapter 7, but for now, you can pencil $1,000 into your startup cost worksheet if you think a tent is a good idea.

If you really have to use the family van/ SUV/truck for your business, you may want to invest in a mobile rig that can be hooked to the back of your vehicle during business hours. These rigs can carry everything you need and may include a water tank, a pressure washer, pressurized hoses, chemical dispensers, and other tools. They run anywhere from $3,000 to $5,000. Add on a mobile wash system for $2,200, and you're ready to detail anything that gets in your way. Other companies sell systems that can be skid-mounted in the back of a truck.

Finally, mobile detailers need a wastewater reclamation system to capture water runoff so chemicals don't wind up in municipal storm sewers. Although this is an EPA requirement, many mobile detailers ignore the law and go on their merry way, polluting the water. But don't do it. In addition to harming Mother Earth, you could be subject to stiff fines if the municipality where you do business finds out you're not reclaiming the water properly. Not to mention it doesn't look very professional working in the center of an office complex parking lot with a lake accumulating around the car you're detailing. Plus, it won't bode well for your reputation or your opportunity to use that location in the future.

Wastewater reclamation systems consist of a flexible tube with a flat bottom that is adhered to surfaces like concrete using a vacuum. This forms an impenetrable barrier where wastewater can collect. This water is then vacuumed up and discharged into a holding tank so it can later be poured into any sanitary sewer—even your toilet. These systems start at around $2,400 for a system that can be used when runoff is in one direction, or $3,400 for a closed-loop system that completely surrounds the vehicle.

Other things you'll need to run a mobile business include office furniture for your home workspace; office equipment and supplies, including a computer, printer, phone, and answering machine; business cards; and uniforms. Each of these items is discussed in the site-based requirements information that follows.

Fixed-Location Bays, Fixtures, and Furniture

In addition to all the equipment you'll need, you have to outfit the facility to make the work areas functional and the customer areas comfortable. For the purpose of this discussion, we'll assume you'll be working in a building that has automotive bays. So the only other requirements are good overhead lighting, plenty of electrical outlets, convenient water sources, and enough floor drains of the correct size to meet code, all of which should be in the facility already if it was previously used to provide automotive services. You'll also need a properly functioning sewer system with a sand trap and oil separator, which is required by local ordinances and the EPA. For a further discussion of these requirements, see Chapter 7.

Finally, it would be much appreciated by your employees if you designate a small area in the service room for breaks. A few chairs and maybe a small table where employees can put down their soft drinks or coffee are all that's necessary for someone taking a break from buffing and polishing duties. Alternatively, you could put a couple of guest chairs in your office for the same purpose, as long as there's enough room and you don't mind sharing the space with chattering breakers. Small refrigerators are relatively inexpensive these days and you might include one in the break room so that employees can bring lunch or snacks.

Smart Tip

Tip...

For a more professional detailing environment, consider installing in-shop detailing workstations like the Chemspense system sold by Detail Plus Car Appearance Systems (www.detailplus.com). It neatly holds a wet-dry vacuum; heated soil extractor; coiled lines for operating pneumatic buffers, shampooers, and orbital waxers; and chemical lines for product dispensing.

Waiting Room Necessities

Even though your work area will be the heart of your operation if you have a fixed location, your waiting room is a very important part of your detail shop. To make it comfortable for anyone who must wait for his/her vehicle, put in three to four matching chairs (the padded vinyl chairs sold as "visitors' chairs" at office supply or restaurant supply stores are a good choice and are quite reasonably priced at about $100 each). Other welcome amenities include a coffeemaker and a table to hold it (about $100 for both at an office supply store), a wall-mounted TV ($150 for a new 19" color TV and $100 for the mounting bracket), and a magazine rack ($100) filled with a variety of reading materials (change them once in a while and don't include only car magazines). A display area for retail products (a simple bookcase or wall-mounted shelves will do) and holders for your service brochure and your business cards are also necessary for the waiting room. (Brochure holders run about $10 each and business card holders are around $5.) You'll also need a stool for behind the service counter ($90). And just in case you're wondering, it's not necessary to have a cash register in most detail shops. People who are spending $150 or more for detailing are more likely to use a credit card or write a check than dole out the cash. You can invest in a locking cash box for your desk drawer, where you can stash checks, credit card slips, and the occasional Jacksons and Grants until you cash out at the end of the business day. Remember, you can make some money on auto-related products, so have items displayed, with a few extras in stock and some change in case someone gives you a $20 for a $10 item.

Finally, the waiting area should be well lit and comfortable, meaning you'll probably want to make sure the air conditioning works during the summer months and that you have some heating in the winter. If possible, try to use some type of soundproofing—or choose a location as far from the bays as possible—so that your customers don't have to hear the noise that you aren't hearing because of your headset.

For your own purposes, and not in the waiting room, you should seriously consider investing in a washer and dryer for on-site laundering of towels, detailing aprons, and other items. The last thing you want to do is take those chemical-laden and dirt-encrusted towels home and wash them in the same machine you use for your Jockeys. A low-end Kenmore washer/dryer pair from Sears will cost only about $500 new, but of course you might also be able to find reliable appliances through the classified ads or a used appliance dealer.

Office Equipment and Furniture

Both onsite and mobile detailers have simple needs when it comes to outfitting an office. In the case of a facility-based detailer, your office will house your computer and a printer for creating receipts, as well as credit card processing equipment. The sole exception to this rule would probably be if your office is located so far away from the waiting room that it would be inconvenient for your customers to wait for you to make the trip there and back. If the office is too far away, you could place the credit card equipment out of sight behind the counter.

Speaking of processing credit card transactions, you have a number of options for handling the task. The most common way is with a point-of-sale (POS) terminal (starting at around $299), coupled with a credit card receipt printer ($195). If space is at a premium, you can opt instead for a terminal like the Hypercom T7P Standard, which has a thermal printer built right in so you don't need a separate receipt printer. This type of POS unit starts at around $329. There are even wireless POS terminals, like the Nurit 3010, that are perfect for mobile detailers. They start at around $995, and you'll need cellular phone service to power them.

Finally, if you don't want to invest in any additional equipment at all, you can purchase PC- or MAC-based POS software that works with your desktop computer. A few packages to check out include PcCharge Pro from GO Software Inc., POSitive Basic from POSitive Software and ICVerify from ICVerify, Inc. For more choices and information about merchant software, you can go to www.merchantwarehouse.com or www.merchantsoft.com.

By the way, all this equipment and software is great, but only if you've established a merchant account that will allow you to use it. A merchant account is an electronic clearinghouse for your credit and debit transactions. Typically it costs $100 to establish a new merchant account, and then you'll pay a variety of fees every month to process transactions through the POS equipment discussed above. See Chapter 13 for a more detailed discussion of merchant accounts.

Your basic office furniture needs will include a desk or computer workstation, a comfortable office chair (preferably one that's ergonomic to minimize back discomfort), and one or two sturdy two-or four-drawer file cabinets. Since your customers will never see your office, feel free to furnish it with inexpensive or secondhand furniture, just as long as it's in good condition and allows you to work efficiently.

If you go new, check out office supply stores like Staples or Office Depot, which sell reasonably priced desks for just $200 to $800, and chairs for $100 to $400. Ready-to-assemble furniture is also quite affordable from places like IKEA. You can also go with used furniture, if it's in good condition, which you can find through newspaper classified ads. A two-drawer, letter-size file cabinet costs as little as $25, although the $100 model may be the better buy because its drawers extend fully, making it easier to remove file folders from the very back. See the Office Equipment Worksheet on page 83

Mobile detailers also need a specific place to handle paperwork and make phone calls, but of course that space will be in your home rather than in a shop. That space should be dedicated just to your business, not shared with an X-box 360 or the laundry machine. Make sure you let your children know this is your special place of business and that your computer, desk, fax machine, etc., are not for their entertainment.

You'll need to choose a home office carefully, so that you have a place in which you can quietly handle all of your paperwork and return phone calls and e-mails to clients and suppliers. If you do not have an extra room, explore the possibilities of a partitioned office space in the basement or even in your bedroom, living room, or foyer, if space allows. Consider ventilation, so you are comfortable in the heat of summer and cold of winter, and make sure you have enough electrical outlets for your computer, printer and so on. Home offices are becoming more and more common, so you will likely find some other homebased office workers in your neighborhood from which you can get tips.

Personal Computer

There's no question that a desktop computer is a necessity for this business. In addition to churning out receipts, you can use a computer to write checks to suppliers, balance your budget, handle bookkeeping and record keeping, create promotional materials, track order, surf for better deals on supplies, and so on.

Computer systems, including the CPU, monitor, keyboard, and a printer can be found for $1,500 by shopping at the major stores such as Best Buy or CompUSA or by going online to Dell, Gateway, Apple, Hewlett-Packard, Compaq, IBM or another leading computer manufacturer. It's advantageous to deal with major name stores and manufacturers for warranties and tech support, which may not be as reliable from small shops.

Whether you are planning to buy a desktop computer or intent upon using the one you already have, you should look for the following:

- Minimum 256 MB of RAM

- At least 120, if not 200 or more gigabytes (GB) of hard drive (the more the merrier, for storage)

- At least 1.5 or 2.0 gigahertz (GHz) processing speed (for moving your business along faster),

- At least two universal USB connections for peripherals, which will typically include your printer and perhaps a scanner

- A DVD drive

- Windows XP operating system. Vista is new, but, thus far, not as "amazing" as billed (and tech staffers have claimed that they are busy trying to solve more Vista problems than those of XP)—which means you can get XP for less money and interface with the many other people who are also not yet taking a chance with Vista.

- An internal modem (all newer computers have internal modems which will get you on the internet).

- 3D Graphics card which will allow you to get the latest software programs and use them to your advantage.

- 5.1 Surround Sound (not essential for your purposes, but always a plus for quality sound, such as some background music while you're in the throws of your workday)

- A firewall and anti-virus software. The firewall should be part of your purchasing deal while anti virus programs are a must today for anyone using the internet for anything. Look for PC-cillin, Norton, or one of the other leading anti-virus programs. Sometimes one will be bundled with the computer package. Make sure to update it often.

Mac or PC?

One of the big decisions you will have to make before buying a computer is whether you want a Mac or a PC. The Mac vs. PC discussion has evolved into many a flame war in internet chat rooms and message boards, so be forewarned when asking a computer enthusiast (a.k.a. Techie) about his or her preference.

You need not argue; both systems will meet your basic requirements. However, the bottom line is basically this:

- Macs can be a little pricier because they are less popular than PCs.
- There are more computer software programs and choices for PCs, although most programs today come in both Mac & PC versions.
- The wider use of PCs means there are far more computer viruses and spyware nightmares for PCs than for Macs
- PCs may be faster, but Macs can be easier for those less versed in computers, as they come with very user-friendly programming.
- Each of their users swear by them.

Smart Tip

Tip...

If you are looking for a Mac, you'll have a variety of options from laptops to the all-in-one style iMac to the new Mac Pro tower. The Leopard operating system is powerful, flexible, and easy to use, and most new Macs will run Windows if you need access to both. Go to the Apple website, www.apple.com, for more on the latest Macs.

Of course the end result will be which you feel comfortable using and what the people around you, and in your field, are using.

If you already have a computer that you like, you can certainly seek more speed, more memory, and/or more hard drive capacity. It's all a matter of your budget and your needs. You want a system that can handle your current software and more, should you opt for new software programs or take on additional responsibilities that require greater speed and more memory.

Laptops and Notebooks

For a mobile detailer, a laptop or notebook may be a good choice, since you'll want to utilize any downtime to catch up on paperwork and you can use your computer to log in customer information right there in your temporary location.

Lightweight models can be had for under $1,000. When shopping for a laptop, look for something that is light, but sturdy enough to withstand some bouncing around as you travel. Try out the trackball and look at the size of the screen—you need to feel comfortable. Popular laptops and notebooks can be found from: Dell, Hewlett Packard, Compaq, Toshiba, IBM, Sony, Gateway, Fujitsu/Fuji, Acer, eMachines, and of course Apple.

Printers

The basic printer choices today are simple—laser or inkjet. Both are sold at price points that makes them consumer friendly. Both are subject to the problems listed above. However, there are significant differences in how they work.

- _The Laser Printer._ It is fast (sometimes printing up to 30 pages per minute), an excellent workhorse for volumes of monochrome (one color/black) work, and the cartridges are easy to replace. Lasers initially cost more than inkjets, but the cartridges are less expensive than ink, making them potentially less expensive per page over time. Lasers don't smudge but they do run through cartridges quickly.

- *The Inkjet Printer.* Inkjets are not as fast as lasers, but can provide quality monochrome documents and are typically much better for color on documents and particularly on photographs. Inkjets are cheaper upfront than most laser printers, but the ink will cost more than the cartridges over time and you will end up spending the same or more.

Consider your printing needs and decide which will be best for you. Printers can run from $200 to $2,000 depending on features. Your needs, however, are the deciding factor. If you anticipate printing numerous four-color fliers and brochures, you may opt for an ink jet. If you need invoices and other materials in a hurry, you'll probably go for a laser printer. Most color laser printers today have pretty good quality as well as speed.

Read up on printers at PC Magazine and other computer websites as well as in chats and on postings, where people tell it like it is. Popular printer models include: Canon, Epson, Oki Data, Brother, Lexmark, and Hewlett Packard.

Cameras—Going Digital

Posting digital photos of your work on your website, or on your brochures, is a major plus for your marketing efforts. Pictures are still worth a thousand words and digital cameras can bring in thousands of dollars, once people can see what you have done. For $400 to $800 you can land a good-quality digital camera. Get a good warranty and make sure tech support exists.

Once the photo is in your computer, you can manipulate it in all sorts of interesting ways, acting as your own photo-finishing expert. You can crop it, expand it, zoom in or out on various features, blur the edges for that shot-through-gauze look, make it look like a watercolor, pastel, or oil painting, ad infinitum. This stuff is not only great for business purposes, it's a heck of a lot of fun! Many digital cameras come complete with photo-finishing software, or you can purchase any number of programs, from Broderbund's Print Shop Deluxe, priced at about $40, to the latest version of Adobe's Photoshop, which costs about $600. Since

Dollar Stretcher

Keep an eye out for what are called "bundled extras" in the computer world, while browsing and comparing prices. Necessary items such as software, ink cartridges, and various peripherals can be part of a deal that might cost several hundred dollars if purchased separately.

your product photos are very important to the success of your business, don't skimp on a good camera or on a software program that lets you highlight your work.

To provide a true example of your talents, take before and after photos.

Software

While there are many general office productivity and business software packages on the market, Microsoft Office and Intuit QuickBooks are the standards. You can buy "suites" (as they are called) that handle a wide range of office functions.

While there are some POS programs available for car washes, there are no specific programs for auto detailing on the market. Since you will not have the same steady flow of business as a car wash, you need not get such an elaborate program. For a more service-oriented program, you might look at Service CEO, which helps you manage everything from marketing to customer calls to invoicing and receivables. This program is also good for managing customer records, schedules, and personnel information

Of course, this will all depend on your needs, computer skills, and level of organization. If you are comfortable with the computer and diligent about record keeping, you can create your own Excel spread sheets and easily maintain such customer and personnel records.

As mentioned earlier (it's important enough to repeat), if you do not already have it, anti-virus protection is a must on any computer, even if you are not online often. PC-cillin, AntiVir, McAfee, and Norton are among the many possibilities.

Fax Machine

Now that computers come equipped with fax cards, full-size fax machines are becoming less common. That's also why the prices have dropped to as little as $150 for a multifunction machine that also scans, copies, and prints. If you decide to install your fax machine on a dedicated telephone line, the installation fee will run $40 to $60, plus you'll incur the cost of the monthly phone service. For the few faxes you will get, the dedicated line isn't worth it. You can always use your regular phone and, when a fax is coming in, have it set up to switch the call to the fax machine. A stand-alone fax machine and a separate printer are your best bet, rather than the combination models, which typically cause you more headaches than they're worth. You can get a decent stand-alone fax machine for $100, or you can buy a fax software program.

Telephones, Answering Machines, and Pagers

Make sure you buy the best model you can afford since you and your staff will be using the phone constantly. A standard two-line speakerphone with auto redial, memory dial, flashing lights, mute button, and other useful features will run $70 to $150, while a top-of-the-line model can cost $250 or more. A great source for high-quality phones is Hello Direct (www.hellodirect.com). You can also find plenty of phones at Staples and other office supply stores.

A stand-alone answering machine costs $40 to $150, while a cordless phone/answering machine combo runs $50 to nearly $200. Buy the best you can afford; it will serve you well. Your other option is voice mail, which can run you $10 to $15 per month.

Although a cell phone isn't really a necessity for a detailer, unless you're going mobile, almost everyone has one these days, so chances are, you do too. If your cell is used strictly for business, it's 100 percent deductible on your business taxes. New cellular service starts at about $20 a month for a minimum number of minutes, to as much as $70 for the Cadillac of phone packages. The cell phone itself will run up to $300 for the coolest models or under $100 for a Plain Jane model.

Finally, pagers are a handy way to keep in touch with your employees, and they're very inexpensive these days. A lot of paging service providers will throw in a basic pager when you activate the service. Otherwise, a new pager costs as little as $30 from sources like Beepers.com (see the Appendix). As with cellular service, there are tons of service plans to choose from.

Backup Power

You should invest in a UPS, or uninterruptible power supply (not to be confused with UPS, the shipping service), for your computer system, especially if you are living in an area where lightning or power surges are frequent. Remember, even a flicker of power loss can shut down your computer or cause you to lose unsaved data. With a UPS in your arsenal, you won't lose power to your computer system when the power in your home or office fails. Instead, the unit sounds a warning, giving you ample time to save your data, log off, and safely shut down your computer.

Copy Machines

Having a copy machine in your office is a real convenience, although not a necessity for most detailers. If you think you need one, pick up a compact personal copier from an office superstore for as little as $150, which gives you just basic copy functions. If you have big jobs, like printing 1,000 fliers, take them someplace like Staples or a local copy shop for reproducing. Supplies you'll need for your copier include copy paper and toner cartridges. Both are readily available from your local office supply store; the cartridges sell for around $90.

Office Supplies

You're going to need a supply of pens, paper, Post-Its®, file folders, and other office supplies to do business. About $30 a month should cover anything you'll need.

Another necessary startup cost is for business cards, brochures, and service menus (a brochure-sized document that has the prices of all the services you offer). A quick-print shop like American Speedy Printing or an online printing company like ColorPrintingCentral.com can design and produce all these items for you. (We've listed a few companies under "Printing Resources" in the Appendix.) To get the most competitive quote, you can use an online source like Print Quote USA. All you do is type in the specs for your job, and the website will do the rest. A casual price survey revealed that 1,000 full-color 8.5-by-11-inch brochures printed on good quality paper can run around $350.

The major office supply stores are a good source for professional-looking yet inexpensive business cards. They start at around $25 for 1,000 one-color business cards on laid stock, which is sturdy and conservative. Don't get too fancy. Provide the basic contact info and, at best, a small graphic of a car. Remember to always have business cards on hand and network regularly.

Security Equipment

If you plan to allow customers to drop off vehicles before the shop opens or the night before they're serviced, you'll need to invest in a reliable security system. Probably the best choice for a detailing shop is a silent alarm, which is connected to a monitoring station that notifies the police when the alarm is tripped. Perimeter or entry alarms sound if someone tries to enter your shop, whereas space protection alarms use infrared beams or motion detectors to detect whether someone is in your facility illegally. The least effective type is local alarms, which aren't connected to an alarm company monitoring station or police department but are loud and can attract unwanted attention—if anyone really cares enough to report the blaring alarm. Whichever system you choose, pick one with a battery or other backup in case of a power failure.

Often a combination of alarm types is necessary to protect your property adequately. A combination package may cost $500 to $2,000, and an installed alarm can run $1,500 to $3,000. Consult the "Security Control Equipment and Systems" category in the Yellow Pages for security system vendors and installers.

Signage

How will people know where you are and what your prices are without proper signage? You will need an exterior sign for a standing location as well as clear signs for exits, fire exits, and your menu of services with the prices or price range (since prices may vary depending on the type of vehicle).

Your outdoor sign, depending on whether you go metal ($2,000+) or with the newer trend in vinyl ($1,000+) is your primary expense in this area. Make sure your sign can be seen from passing motorists and do not clutter it up with extraneous matter.

Comparison shopping for signs is like everything else. Look for quality product samples at good prices and a company that can get the sign in front of your business on time. Get references. Sign-a-Rama is a national signage company at www.sarsign.com. You can look online or in the Yellow Pages for a nearby sign company.

Research city ordinances to determine what size and types of signs you can put up outside. You will also need numerous interior signs, which can be purchased for a total of $500 to $1,000. Take your time and determine your needs, then carefully plan a menu sign that is clear and easy to read. Don't forget to factor signage in as a startup expense.

The Moment of Truth

Take a look at the worksheet "Dealing Equipment and Supplies" (page 80) for some numbers to give you an idea of how it would look to get started. Let's begin with your detailing equipment and supplies for a standing operation. Some of the following apply for a mobile detailer as well; however, a fully equipped mobile detailing trailer can be purchased for around $5,500 to $8,000. Of course if you elect to buy a truck or van, you will still need some of the accessories listed at the beginning of the chapter, which can run another $3,000 beyond the cost of the vehicle.

Mobile detailers also need to add a water reclamation system, which can run about $2,500. A fixed location will need one as well, so if there is not one on the premises, you can also add $2,500 to your costs. This would bring the total for a fixed location up to roughly $14,000 and a mobile detailer may top $10,000.

A sample worksheet for your expenses for office equipment and supplies follows on page 82. For a mobile auto detailer, you can deduct waiting room furniture, and unless you plan to take some items along with you to sell, you can skip the line for inventory of salable car items. However, you will likely need to have many of the worksheet items in your home office setting.

Startup costs (see page 84) for a standing detail business with two employees should begin at roughly $66,000, plus you'll want to have at least $10,000 in available cash on hand at all times. A mobile detail operation can eliminate employees, add the purchase of a truck (a total difference of less $24,000), deduct most signage costs ($2,500), and mortgage ($7,500). A mobile detailer will also be able to buy a fully equipped trailer for $6,000 to $9,000. Therefore, mobile detailers can typically start up for anywhere from $25,000 to $35,000.

Detailing Equipment and Supplies

Air compressor	$400
Random orbital polisher	$300 **
Variable-speed rotary buffer/polisher	$400 **
Pressure washer	$1,500
125-gallon water tank	$290
5-gallon stainless-steel tank sprayer	$350 **
Ozone Generator	$600
Carpet extractor	$1,300
Wet-dry vacuum	$250
Vapor steam cleaner	$1,200
Interior dryer	$175
Creeper	$170
Temperature gauge	$80
Digital electronic paint-thickness gauge	$500
Magnifier loupe	$15
Towels	$100
Towel wringer	$120
Generator	$1,600
Miscellaneous detailing tools	$600
Miscellaneous detailing supplies	$1,000
Washer, dryer	$500
Total	**$11,450**

*** For a quantity of two*

Detailing Equipment and Supplies Worksheet

Air compressor	
Random orbital polisher	
Variable-speed rotary buffer/polisher	
Pressure washer	
125-gallon water tank	
5-gallon stainless-steel tank sprayer	
Ozone Generator	
Carpet extractor	
Wet-dry vacuum	
Vapor steam cleaner	
Interior dryer	
Creeper	
Temperature gauge	
Digital electronic paint-thickness gauge	
Magnifier loupe	
Towels	
Towel wringer	
Generator	
Miscellaneous detailing tools	
Miscellaneous detailing supplies	
Washer, dryer	
Any other equipment you deem necessary for your detailing operation...	
Total	

Office Equipment and Supplies

Computer, printer	$2,000
UPS	$125
Fax machine	$130
Printer and extra toner cartridge	$400
Phone expenses, including cell phone, answering machine, or initial service fee and pagers	$600
Calculator	$25
Security system	$2,000
Software programs	$500
Office furniture	$1,200
Office supplies, including business cards	$500
Service brochures	$400
Waiting room furniture/equipment (includes chairs or sofa, TV, coffee maker & TV rack)	$1,000
Initial stock of detailing supplies	$1,500
Inventory of salable car items	$1,000
Total	**$11,380**

Office Equipment and Supplies Worksheet

Computer, printer	
UPS	
Fax machine	
Printer and extra toner cartridge	
Phone expenses, including cell phone, answering machine or initial service fee and pagers	
Calculator	
Security system	
Software programs	
Office furniture	
Office supplies, including business cards	
Service brochures	
Waiting room furniture/equipment (includes chairs or sofa, TV, coffee maker & TV rack)	
Initial stock of detailing supplies	
Inventory of salable car items	
Total	

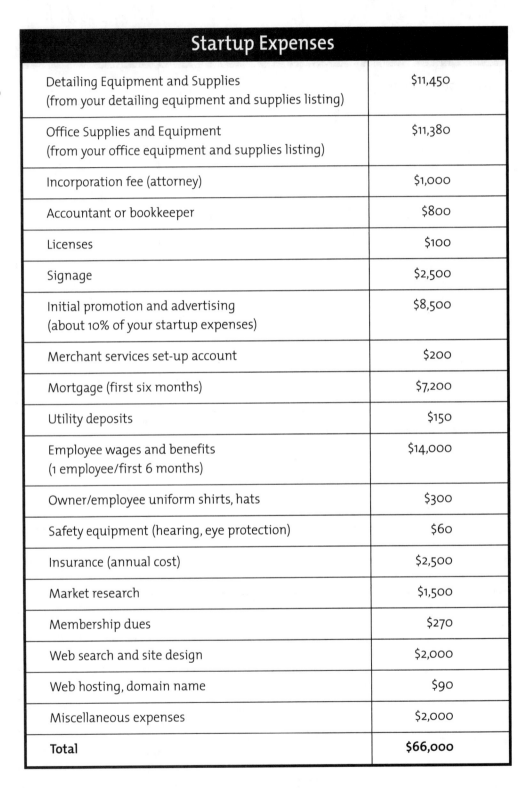

Startup Expenses	
Detailing Equipment and Supplies (from your detailing equipment and supplies listing)	$11,450
Office Supplies and Equipment (from your office equipment and supplies listing)	$11,380
Incorporation fee (attorney)	$1,000
Accountant or bookkeeper	$800
Licenses	$100
Signage	$2,500
Initial promotion and advertising (about 10% of your startup expenses)	$8,500
Merchant services set-up account	$200
Mortgage (first six months)	$7,200
Utility deposits	$150
Employee wages and benefits (1 employee/first 6 months)	$14,000
Owner/employee uniform shirts, hats	$300
Safety equipment (hearing, eye protection)	$60
Insurance (annual cost)	$2,500
Market research	$1,500
Membership dues	$270
Web search and site design	$2,000
Web hosting, domain name	$90
Miscellaneous expenses	$2,000
Total	**$66,000**

Startup Expenses Worksheet

Detailing Equipment and Supplies (from your detailing equipment and supplies listing)	
Office Supplies and Equipment (from your office equipment and supplies listing)	
Incorporation fee (attorney)	
Accountant or bookkeeper	
Licenses	
Signage	
Initial promotion and advertising (about 10% of your startup expenses)	
Merchant services set-up account	
Mortgage (first six months)	
Utility deposits	
Employee wages and benefits (2 employees/first 6 months)	
Owner/employee uniform shirts, hats	
Safety equipment (hearing, eye protection)	
Insurance (annual cost)	
Market research	
Membership dues	
Web search and site design	
Web hosting, domain name	
Miscellaneous expenses	
Total	

Low Budget Startup: Is It Possible?

Let's say you can't get the $65,000 to $75,000 you might need to open a fixed location detailing shop with three people (yourself + two) or the $30,000 it might take to really launch a full-fledged mobile business, what do you do? It is possible to start a detailing business on a shoestring budget.

You can get started by operating with a few tools, and offering a few basic (popular) services, such as a basic wash and vacuuming. This is minimal equipment that you can keep in your van or car, and you can start your business for less than $1,000. Yes, you should add some minimal insurance to cover yourself.

If you are good at what you do, then you can spread the word locally by word of mouth and with some signs at gas stations and businesses in the neighborhood. Post a sign in the window of your car and tell your friends, family, and neighbors about your service and ask them to spread the word. Drive around in a well-detailed vehicle; people will notice the shine on your car and ask where it came from. Remember, you can be your own best marketer.

Once you get business, be meticulous and charge competitive rates to show that you are every bit as good as anyone else. At home, use some basic computer programs, even a regular notebook (not the laptop kind) to keep track of supplies, customers, etc.

Send out reminder cards to regular customers or ask for their e-mail addresses and send an occasional e-mail. Remember, as is the case with most businesses, 80 percent of your business will come from repeat customers. So start making friends with your customers and keep in touch with them.

Now, perhaps you're up to a few thousand dollars, and you can get started. Also, if you choose to affiliate with a local business in town, you can build a business of steady clients by giving them a piece of the action. Typically, this will be a gas station or car wash that does not already have a detailer. Don't give them exclusive rights to your services, however, so that you can also spend some days on the road, or in your driveway, detailing.

A Garage for All Seasons:
Housing Your Business

Up to this point, we've discussed business basics that could apply to both mobile detailers and site-based detailers. Now let's zero in on the main difference between the two types of detailers: the actual space where you'll do business, whether it's outdoor space or a brick-and-mortar facility, as well as the places you can store your equipment and supplies.

▲

Mobile Machinations

As we mentioned earlier, if you're interested in a low-cost startup, then mobile is the way to go because no facility is necessary. A mobile detailer's major fixed costs generally consist only of detailing equipment and some form of transportation (van, truck, SUV, or trailer) to get the equipment where the business is. But you'll still need a place to park all that equipment and your vehicle when they're not in use. And by the way, that shady spot on the street in front of your house is not an option—many cities and townships have ordinances that prohibit parking commercial vehicles and/or equipment rigs in the street.

The garage at your home is the logical place to store everything if you can spare the space. All you'll need is some steel shelving from a home improvement store so you can organize polishes, towels, and other supplies and keep them close at hand. To get your rig off the street when it's not in use, consider renting a unit in a self-storage facility. A space as small as 150 square feet, which is about the size of a large bedroom, should be sufficient for all your equipment and supplies. If you want to park your entire trailer inside, however, you'll need about 200 square feet (the size of a small one-car garage). Self-storage rental runs about $100 to $400 a month, depending on the location and size of the facility.

Because unexpected rainfall, surprise snow flurries, and extremely hot weather can adversely affect the way polishes and finishes seal on the vehicles you detail, you might consider investing in a portable pop-up tent that you can set up easily at the first sign of any weather that threatens your hard work. These canopies are so lightweight and easy to transport that some manufacturers recommend adding tent sandbags to make sure the tent itself doesn't take flight. A 10-by-20-foot tent that covers a 200 square foot area runs around $1,000, and a set of six ready-to-use sandbags is about $80. The minimal shelter provided by this type of canopy also is effective for protecting yourself against UVA and UVB rays, which is always advisable because too much sun exposure can increase your risk of developing skin cancer.

A canopy can also come in handy for setting up a temporary detailing location, such as in a parking lot or office complex, where you can service drive-up customers. (Just be sure to obtain permission from the parking or building

> **Beware!**
> More care and maintenance is needed for the tools and equipment used by a mobile operator than those used in a facility-based detailing business. Specialty equipment like compressors, power generators, and water reclamation equipment all need regular maintenance to make sure they don't go down when you have a book filled with appointments.

management company before unfurling your canopy.) Other places where a temporary location might work are swap meets and classic car shows—basically, any place where car aficionados congregate. If you have the option of having the canopy emblazoned with your company name, take it. It's great advertising at a reasonable cost. Remember to look for car shows in advance so that you can pay to be included and they will save a space for you.

To set up a temporary location, you'll need the same equipment as a mobile detailer, including water tanks, a power generator, and other accoutrements. Also, like a mobile detailer, you may have to relocate occasionally to get enough business. On the other hand, you won't spend as much time every day driving from job site to job site as you do when you're truly mobile.

Dollar Stretcher

If you have the time and inclination, you can make sandbags instead of buying them. Buy ready-made canvas or burlap feed bags from a farm supply store, fill them with sandbox sand (often available at home improvement stores), turn the open side under twice, and staple them securely closed.

Shop Talk

A lot of detailers—including those who work in northern climates, where the weather can be fickle or downright lousy three-quarters of the year—choose to work out of a specialized detailing shop. The disadvantage is there are many more startup costs when you have a fixed location, plus someone has to be at the shop all the time in case a customer stops by for unscheduled work, to make an appointment, or to buy do-it-yourself detailing products. The advantage is you could make a lot more money than you could as a mobile detailer, assuming you pick a good location and hire the right employees. Even in northern locations, where the detailing business drops off in the winter, you can find work among those auto aficionados who keep their rides showroom-perfect no matter what the weather (or perhaps because of the weather) as well as from dealers who use detailers to prep new vehicles and restore used and off-lease vehicles. As mentioned previously, there's even a thriving market for boat and airplane detailing; winter might be a good time to promote that part of your business. And let's not forget snowmobiles.

Location, Location, Location

Your detailing shop should be located in a commercial area that's easily accessible by highway or byway, preferably one that has plenty of traffic because that gives you added visibility. The building should have sufficient adjacent parking if at all possible, and the surrounding area should be well-maintained, well-lighted, and safe. Of course, such a business will have to fit within the zoning ordinances.

Another desirable location is an auto mall, both because the new- and used-car dealers that anchor such malls are often frequent consumers of detailing work themselves and because there will be a steady stream of car shoppers in the area who could be prospective detailing customers. Likewise, a location in a mini-mall that has non-competing automotive businesses, like tire stores, brake shops, vehicle alarm installers, and so on, can bring you great visibility and increased sales. Finally, a free-standing building located on the perimeter or "outlot" of a shopping center or mall, like those used by the national quick-lube franchises, could be an ideal choice. Look for a location that meets your personal needs as well by being within a reasonable drive from your home.

Building Basics

Your first decision concerning your detailing facility should be whether you're up to the challenge of renovating an existing building or whether you'd prefer to move into a garage or gas station that's either defunct or for sale. (We won't even consider building a new facility as an option—it's simply too expensive for most new detailing entrepreneurs.) Renovation can be very expensive, so generally speaking it's better to look for a building that previously served as an automotive service provider, such as a garage. The good news is that a lot of the infrastructure you'll need, including automobile bays, special electrical connections, and maybe even fixtures (such as a service counter) may come with the building. The bad news is that there could be a really good reason why the previous owner moved out, like too much competition in the area, the location is crummy, or the previous owner had a poor reputation in the community. The same goes for a detailing or other automotive-type business that's currently in business but is up for sale.

If you're seriously interested in taking over an existing or now-defunct detailing shop, garage, or gas station, try to find out why it's on the block. If the business for sale is a detailing shop that's still operating, observe its activities for a few days, noting daily volume and clientele. Also, determine the worth of any equipment or fixtures that will be left behind and decide whether you'll be able to use it. Finally, consider remodeling costs vs. the cost of starting with a blank slate in a different facility. Find out the seller's asking price and review the valuation of the property and what comes as part of the deal.

Using due diligence, you can find out:

- how much direct competition is in the area
- what prices comparable businesses in the region have sold for
- what changes, if any, are anticipated for the neighborhood

- if there are any tax, zoning, environmental, or other laws that may be passed and become legislation in the near future, and see which ones might affect your business.

A word of warning about shuttered gas stations: During the Reagan administration, legislation was signed into law requiring owners of gas stations and other facilities that have underground storage tanks to monitor them for leakage and properly clean up contaminated sites. Tanks that were found to be leaking had to be permanently closed and the soil decontaminated, and, not surprisingly, the cost of doing this drove some service stations out of business. So before you purchase an abandoned gas station, ask about the condition of the underground storage tanks and the owner's compliance with EPA requirements, including monitoring and soil testing. The EPA estimates that 225,000 sites in the United States are contaminated by petroleum leakage, and you don't want to get stuck with a hefty bill for cleanup. For more information about the initiative to clean up underground storage tanks (known as the Brownfield law), check out the EPA's website at www.epa.gov/swerust1, or call the EPA hotline at (800) 424-9346.

Brownfields are a good possibility for a detailing business because you get an old abandoned building for a fairly low cost investment and can set it up as you like. The National Brownfield Association (brownfieldassociation.org) can provide a wealth of information. The first step is to have a complete feasibility study of the property done, so you know what you are up against. If there is not a high "contamination clean-up cost," you may be able to get a very good deal on such a property.

One potential problem with existing sites is that they may lack a properly functioning sewer system with a sand trap and oil separator, all of which are required by the EPA and many government agencies. All businesses are prohibited from discharging contaminants into the sewer system, so the sand trap and oil separator are required to remove sludge from water and divert it into a collection tank before the water is discharged into the sewer. The trouble is that it's not uncommon for buildings that have been used for automotive services to lack this very expensive system.

"It can cost a small fortune to retrofit a shop that doesn't have a working system, so I wouldn't even look at a shop that wasn't set up right," says Tom Schurmann, a 32-year detailing veteran in Lakewood, Colorado. "Some detailers ignore the rules, then find themselves in a major mess with city officials, the EPA, and a multitude of government agencies."

To find an existing location for sale or lease (with or without the proper environmental protection equipment), check the advertising section of your local newspaper, or contact a commercial real estate broker or agent. Find out who pays the broker/agent commission before you get started. As for financing, we'll discuss how to get the money to buy or start a business in Chapter 13, once you have already determined that this may be the right business for you.

Buying Vs. Leasing

When you start looking at buildings, you'll find that the terms may vary widely, from adjustable rate mortgages to short-term leases. In many cases, buying a building outright brings more benefits, including giving you more latitude when it comes to renovations and allowing you to control fixed costs like overhead, utilities, and (within reason) the terms of the mortgage. You'll also have the tax advantages of owning the building.

Leasing a freestanding building gives you some of the same advantages as buying, although you will have a landlord to deal with. But you can usually negotiate favorable terms upfront, so leasing is certainly a viable option.

At the Very Lease

Leasing can be an excellent way to go if you don't want to own the property and secure a mortgage. Depending on the real estate market, you may find this a better, lower-cost alternative. In addition, leasing allows you to pick up and move out if the facility doesn't meet your needs or if you decide to take your show on the road.

Leases are typically either a flat fee, in which you pay a specific amount, or adjusted by the cost of living as determined by government figures. Of course, the first thing to remember is that no matter what the landlord tells you, there's no such thing as a "standard lease." That's a line used to get you to glance over the lease without reading it, which is a VERY bad idea. Leases have various clauses and they can all be negotiated unless government laws state otherwise.

The areas you want to pay the closest attention to are the specific lease terms regarding the length of the lease, when the rent can be raised, and by how much. Make sure any rent hikes are spelled out in advance. You will also want to examine the use clause, which signifies what the space can and cannot be used for. Review such a clause carefully. Landlords want to protect their property, but you need to make sure that his or her interpretation of usage does not infringe upon your use of the space to adequately conduct your business.

An important area of concern, and often contention, is defining exactly what you are and are not responsible for. In an auto mall, or a shopping center, how much will you need to pay for the upkeep of common areas? What about parking in the lot? Do you have a certain amount of spaces for people who are waiting? Do you pay extra for these and is it written into the lease? Are there rules and regulations about the hours that you can be open and the signage that you use?

Buying means, of course, a major outlay of funding, even for a down payment. It also requires that you establish a strong credit rating in order to find a mortgage lender and get a deal. Before you consider buying, you will probably want to get your feet wet in the detailing industry by working at someone else's location, going mobile, or leasing for a couple of years. You will also need to know the status of the real estate market in a given region. Buying a property means making a major investment in your business and adding on a significant asset. This is more appealing in a real estate market that has a bright future. Therefore, you need to get a feel for the trends and growth of an area before buying into it. If you see homes and stores being built in an area, and it is not a commuter area (like Manhattan), you may see the forthcoming increase in automobiles as a good opportunity. However, if the economy of an area is

---

Make sure you cover all restrictions and all payments that you are expected to make before leasing a location in a multi-purpose center.

While this is not all that common among auto detailing businesses, some leases allow you to rent out space (or sublet) to other businesses until you have the funding to fill up the location. This too needs to be in the lease and agreed upon in advance by both parties.

If you are looking into a multi-purpose facility such as an auto mall, you will also want to discuss adding an exclusivity clause. Such a clause basically helps you limit competing businesses from opening up next door. Typically in a mall, you may expect to have no direct competition and this agreement can ensure that no other auto detailing business opens in the same mall.

Another major concern today is security. If a clause is included regarding securing your premises, then you need to evaluate it carefully. There are several questions to which you will want to find answers, such as

- ○ Who is responsible for securing the premises?
- ○ What does "security" constitute?
- ○ Can you install a security system?
- ○ Does the landlord have access to your leased area?

The key to successfully leasing a commercial property is to review—with an attorney—all of the possibilities. Ultimately you want no surprises. You want to make sure that all of your business needs are covered and that you can run your business comfortably for the term of the lease.

Finally, make sure you are listed properly as one of the parties on the signed agreement. Many people do not take a close look at this, but it can be important in the future. For example, if partners are opening a business together, do they both have their names on the lease? Should they separate, this can be an important point of contention. Review with your attorney how the "parties" should be listed and have your attorney review the lease with you.

Smart Tip

Tip...

When negotiating a lease for a lot of money, don't go it alone. Hire an attorney to look over the terms so you don't get burned. Among the things you'll want to negotiate are which additions or renovations are needed before the property is acceptable and the timetable for getting them done.

on the down side, and there are many businesses moving elsewhere, you may get a good price on a building, but it may not be worth buying.

Leasing does not give you the asset, but it also does not require as extensive funding. Many entrepreneurs in all types of businesses start off by leasing—some stay with leases because they can get a prime location that they otherwise could not afford to purchase. Some opt to move to owning their own place, which allows for more personal options and gives you ownership of a property.

Layout

A detailing facility has to be highly functional and have plenty of room to spread out in. Toward that end, you'll want to find a building of around 2,000 square feet, which is enough space for two to three bays. If the building was previously used for a garage or other automotive-based business and has hoists, so much the better. But a building with standard service bays will work just fine. About 75 percent of the floor space should be allocated to the work area, which you'll want to line with shelving to store products and equipment. The rest of the building should be allocated for a manager's office (large enough for a small desk and a chair), a customer service area where clients can sit down until their vehicle is completed, a unisex restroom, and a storage area. You'll also have to find a place to stash the washer and dryer you'll need (you'll be doing a lot of towels, buffer pads, and other laundry). The trick is to find a place where the agitating and spinning won't be too noisy.

If you find the right size garage in a great location, but it doesn't have all these basic necessities, you should strongly consider doing some remodeling to include them. You'll find a sample layout for a 2,000-square-foot facility on page 95.

You'll want to keep all areas of the shop scrupulously clean. Seeing a cluttered detailing area or a messy manager's office could make customers question just how meticulous you'll be when detailing their prized rides. Likewise, the customer area should be neat and brightly lit, and the furniture must be comfortable and in good repair. Also allot a small corner of the

Smart Tip

Tip...

A bare concrete floor is acceptable for your waiting area if it's unstained and clean, but a durable floor covering like indoor-outdoor carpeting or tile is a good alternative. Be sure to select flooring in a neutral tone that will conceal dirt and blend with the wall color.

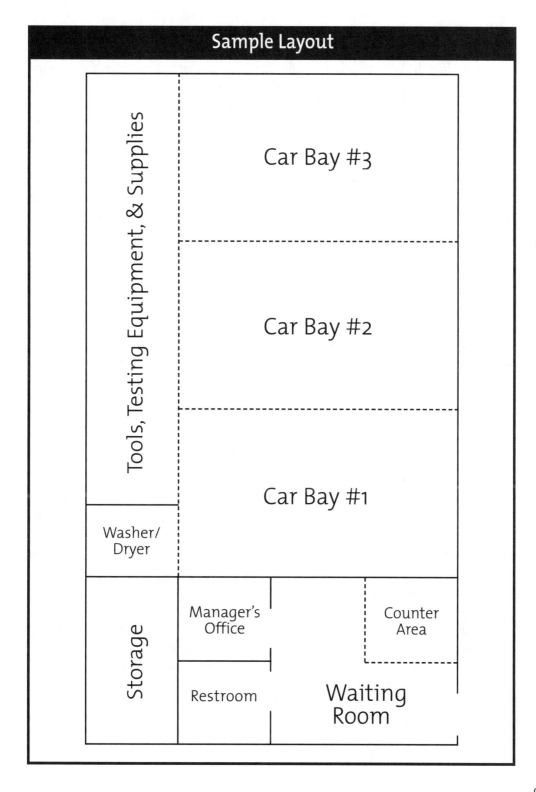

Sample Layout

Tools, Testing Equipment, & Supplies

Car Bay #3

Car Bay #2

Car Bay #1

Washer/ Dryer

Storage

Manager's Office

Restroom

Counter Area

Waiting Room

waiting room for a coffeemaker or coffee service, a complimentary amenity that will be much appreciated by clients. Just be sure to keep an eye on coffee levels and make a new pot when the brew runs low. Finally, hang a couple of framed prints (of hot cars, of course—or better still, cars you've detailed) and place a potted plant or two in the waiting area to make it look fresh and comfortable, particularly if you're after an upscale clientele. This might be a working garage, but you also want to show a sense of style. Making a good impression on discriminating customers is an important part of doing business.

A sampling of any retail products you sell should be displayed in this area. You can use steel shelving from any home improvement store, but you might consider buying standard retail display racks instead, since they look more professional. Unless you have a clear view into your customer waiting area, you might not want to put a lot of product on the shelves. Easy access can be tempting for someone who can't control the urge to help him- or herself to the products. Instead, keep your overstock in your work area and bring out fresh supplies only when customers are ready to pay for them.

Karen Duncan of Union Park Appearance Care Center in Wilmington, Delaware, took detail shop retailing to a new level—she sold greeting cards in the waiting room of her previous shop. "I used to stock cute cards with cars on them from smaller companies like Blue Mountain," she says. "People waiting for their cars would buy them— even the men. A lot of times they'd spent as much as $10 to $15 at a time. Eventually people started to stop by just to buy cards, so I added car models, mugs, key chains, and special-order items like sheepskin covers, and they all did well."

Sign of the Times

As mentioned in the last chapter, signage is also important. You'll want a large, pro-fessional-looking sign that announces to the world that you're in business. It should give the name of your detailing shop in letters that are large enough to be seen by passing motorists. If your primary sign can't be seen from all directions (for instance, if your building is on a corner), you should have a sign on each side of the building where traffic passes. Make sure the print is not too elaborate and can be easily read. Sometimes too fancy can mean lost business.

Signage is one of the more costly startup expenses, but it's truly worth the price. Just be sure to check with the local zoning commission before erecting a sign, even if you're simply replacing the one that was already on the building. Although there's lit-tle doubt you'll be able to put something on the front of your building, sign ordi-nances do change. The last thing you want to do is spend big bucks on a great sign only to find out it's over the size limit or the city fathers don't like the particular shade of puce you've chosen.

Finding
Good Help

Are you looking for new challenges, high adventure, and great excitement in your day-to-day business operations? Then hire a few employees.

Employees are integral to making your detailing business grow and expand into new service areas. They allow you to put more mobile detailing vehicles on the road and more bodies in the shop. But they also can be high maintenance and temperamental while they're helping you achieve greater things in your detailing kingdom.

If you're planning to be a solo operator in your new business venture, you can skip ahead to Chapter 9, which deals with professional development opportunities that can make you a better detailer. But if you think you may need additional help now or in the near future, even if it's only a part-time person to vacuum cars and recondition leather seats while you're tinting windshields, then read on.

Labor Pool

Any person who owns and operates a small business won't hesitate to tell you that one of the most challenging aspects of being a business owner is hiring and retaining good employees. The process of hiring can be daunting if you've never done it before, plus the auto detailing industry seems to experience a higher employee turnover than the average service industry. This might be because the "helper" jobs tend to pay minimum wage, and although these employees might be passionate about cars, they may be more passionate about making 25 cents an hour more at the local quick-lube joint. Also, with the exception of a few training programs, a handful of courses on videotape and some online courses, such as an online "detailing college," there isn't an education track for becoming a detailer like there is for becoming an auto mechanic or a computer technician. As a result, you'll probably find yourself constantly looking for eager, bright, and motivated workers who can be trained in the basic techniques of detailing.

Hiring inexperienced help isn't necessarily a bad thing. Some detailers prefer to hire people who don't have detailing experience. "It's more difficult to change the habits that employees learned elsewhere than it is to teach them how to clean cars my way," says Dave Echnoz of 14/69 Carwash Supercenter in Fort Wayne, Indiana.

Certainly for some tasks, such as clean up, taking reservations and other non-hands-on car-related tasks, great skills are not required. However, for the actual detailing work, a lot rides on the skills of your employees. Not only are they the frontline representatives of the business, their ability and talent, as well as their attitudes, work ethic, and attention to detail, will influence every aspect of operations, from the client retention rate to the bottom line. For these reasons, you'll want to select your employees very, very carefully.

"I look for the person who has a mind-set to be on time and doesn't think the world owes

Smart Tip

It's usually better not to hire family or friends. If they don't work out, you'll have to fire them, and that could create a very uncomfortable situation around the dinner table. The sole exception might be your spouse, who's supposed to love you no matter what. Just don't let your marriage suffer as a result of your business.

him a living," says Mike Myers of Gem Auto Appearance Center in Waldorf, Maryland. "Then I try to instill my own philosophy and teach them what works for me in today's business climate. When it really clicks and someone gets it, it makes you proud."

The Usual Suspects

There are two types of employees you're most likely to need as a new detailer. The first is the detailing technician who will do everything from emptying ashtrays to putting away new shipments of wax and tire dressing. At least initially, you'll want to handle the more difficult tasks yourself. According to Prentice St. Clair of Detail in Progress in San Diego, the average vehicle has at least ten different types of surfaces that need to be maintained, and until you've had a chance to work with a new employee and train him/her on the proper use of equipment and chemicals used for each of these surfaces, don't entrust a customer's car to that person. Period. The technician also can pick up and deliver vehicles to customers' homes and, once trained, can take a mobile van on the road to find work. For this reason, you should make a driver's license, and a good driving record, conditions of employment for your technicians. Technicians earn anywhere from minimum wage to $12 an hour. Adding incentives for superior work can be an effective way to motivate a good employee to greatness.

The second type of employee you might consider hiring is an assistant manager. Now you're probably thinking, "I can hardly pay myself! How can I afford a manager?"

An assistant manager isn't for every detailing business. But if your operation is so successful that you need to hire someone more experienced right away to help with the flotilla of vehicles you detail, then an assistant manager is a good option. In exchange for a title and a little more money than the average technician gets, you'll get someone who can hit the ground rolling, so to speak. In addition to detailing and picking up and delivering vehicles, this person can assist with paperwork, reconcile the cash drawer, make bank deposits, and so on. If possible, look for someone who has worked in an automotive environment because he/she will understand your business and your clientele better. For the extra assistance this person will provide, you should pay $10 to $15 an hour. Look at the going rate for such employees in your region. Try to stay competitive in your market in order to get better candidates.

Start your search for employees with the right stuff in the advertising section of your local newspaper. Instead of just placing a line ad, which is one of those three-to-five-line ads that gets lumped in with all the other help-wanted ads, request an ad with a box around it to make it stand out. If your newspaper has a section devoted to automotive industry jobs—with everything from managers to mechanics—you'll want to place your ad there. You'll find a sample classified ad on page 100.

Be aware that a one-time insertion probably isn't going to be enough to find the right candidate(s). Ask about the newspaper's rate for running the ad three or four

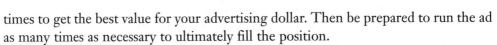

Sample Classified Ad

Automotive Detailer Wanted

Do you love washing and waxing your car until it shines like new?

Then *Great Lakes Automotive Detailing* could have the right job for you! As an auto detailer, you'll take care of all kinds of vehicles, both inside and out. No experience necessary. Valid driver's license and a clean driving record a must. We offer competitive wages and paid vacation after one year.

Call Daniel at (555) 555-0000.

times to get the best value for your advertising dollar. Then be prepared to run the ad as many times as necessary to ultimately fill the position.

You can be like one of Prentice St. Clair's detailing associates and run your ad continuously. He has four mobile units and keeps his help-wanted ad running all the time. He treats his search for employees like a normal part of his operation, not a crisis. He just keeps calling the next person on the list. Over time, this also serves as an ad for his business as people see the name repeatedly.

You can look into web-based job boards like Monster.com, but keep in mind that it is national in scope, so you may get responses from all over the place, making it time consuming to narrow down those that are nearby. Be sure to include your city and state in the ad so you don't have applicants from Jasper, Indiana, applying in vain for your detailing job in Walla Walla, Washington. Your best bet is looking for locally based newspapers or websites that draw most of their visitors from your geographic area.

Keep in mind that when writing out classified ads, you should try to keep the word count down since most papers charge more for extra words above the first 25 or 50, depending on the paper.

Back to School

After the newspaper, probably your next richest source of detailing talent will be found at the local high school or even a community college (especially if it offers training for automotive careers, including auto mechanics). R. L. "Bud" Abraham, president of Detail Plus Car Appearance Systems in Portland, Oregon, recommends contacting these facilities and arranging to participate in their Career Day events, during which students meet with people from a wide variety of industries to get them thinking about a future career. "Also, many high schools have work release programs for vocational studies students who don't plan to attend college," Abraham says. "If you can formalize a training program of your own, it will serve as a shoo-in to get all the good candidates you need."

If the students you meet are at least 18 (and can prove it) and are interested in a job, take their names and arrange an interview in person at your shop right away. If you're mobile, ask prospects to meet you at a job site or other neutral location. Even though 16-year-olds may work legally in some parts of the country, you may find that they are not mature enough for the job, and, in fact, they may not have enough upper-body strength to handle power tools. Of course it depends on the individual student.

The Little Details

It should go without saying that you want employees who are well-groomed. Since an employee's appearance is a reflection on the capability of your staff and the quality of your services, their appearance should be clean-cut, neat, and professional. (See Chapter 6 for a brief discussion on the merits of having a uniform program.) Long hair on men is fine as long as it's neatly secured away from the face during business hours, if only because it could get caught in the equipment with painful results. As for trendy "body wear" like multiple piercings and tattoos, if you eliminate any young person who expresses him/herself that way, you may not have any candidates to choose from. As long as such personal expressions of individuality don't detract from the person's detailing ability, they shouldn't be a problem, although if the tattoo is profane, you might want to ask if he/she would mind keeping it covered during business hours.

Finally, it's a plus if the technician is friendly and has a good gift of gab, and patience and careful attention to detail are musts.

Taking the Plunge

Just as candidates need to prepare before going on job interviews, you also need to be prepared as well. To make your life easier, you might print up some basic job application forms, in which you can ask for basic information, such as name, address, home phone, and cell phone numbers, as well as job history and education. You can ask if someone is over 18 years of age, but not an individual's age if they are over 18. You can purchase blank application forms at office supply stores, a package of 100 runs about $8. If you create your own forms, keep them simple and straightforward, leaving other questions for the interview. Prior to interviewing a job candidate, you should review the person's resume and list some questions that you want to ask. Although you want to ascertain information, you don't want to fire questions at someone, but instead try to create a relaxed atmosphere in which each candidate can explain why he or she would be a good choice to work in your facility. Since many resumes for young candidates will not have much experience listed on them, you are better off asking about

> **Bright Idea**
>
> When prospecting for employees at high school career events, bring informational brochures about your business, a card with your website address, and some advertising specialty items like pencils imprinted with your business name. Even if the student doesn't come to you for a job, that pencil may get around and spark someone else's interest in your business.

detailing skills and previous experience in general. As for references, it is important that you check them carefully. You want to get a general idea of the character, reliability and overall personality of the potential employee.

In a world where employee theft is a rising concern for most business owners, you have the right to be concerned. However, you need not express this to what may be an honest person sitting in front of you. Therefore, along with checking references and possibly contacting previous employers, you might have a 30- to 90-day trial period as a condition of employment. During that time, you can evaluate a person's natural aptitude for the work and his/her dependability.

Interviews should be held in your office or at a neutral facility, such as a coffee shop during non-busy hours. It's advisable to space interviews out so that you have a chance to take some notes on each candidate after he or she leaves. You should also not schedule more than five or six interviews at one time.

As for questions to ask, you'll want to ask questions that touch on general topics like the person's background and interests so you'll want to know about what else he/she has done as a way to gauge that person's suitability for the detailing job. It's also helpful to have a prepared job description that can be given to the candidate. It should include a brief description of the work to be performed, the employee's responsibilities, and the additional support this person is expected to provide (such as answering the phone when the owner is out getting coffee or sweeping up at the end of the day). This is especially important because a lot of people have the mistaken idea that detailing means adding pinstripes or other custom details to a vehicle. You'll want to make it clear that detailing is about restoring and preserving, not customizing.

During the interview, outline the job responsibilities and your expectations, then allow the candidate to do most of the talking. As you listen, watch body language. A confident person will sit up straight in the chair and make direct eye contact with you. In addition, someone who is both articulate and friendly will probably be good with customers.

It's possible that you'll make a decision whether to hire someone at the initial meeting, but it's better to wait until you've checked references before actually hiring anyone. You can let the applicants know the pay rate so that if it is not enough for the individual, you can cut down on the time and effort it takes to check references.

The Benefits of Belonging

It's becoming more common for even the smallest businesses to offer certain benefits to full-time employees as a way to retain them. Health insurance is probably not an option for most detailers because it's too expensive, but offering a perk like one week paid vacation after a year's service, a few personal days, or some scheduling flexibility (especially with students who may have midterm or final exams) can make employees happier and induce them to stick with you, especially if the competition isn't offering similar benefits. Incentives can also be very motivational. For some creative ideas on building employee morale, read "Pump 'Em Up" below.

Taxing Issues

No discussion of employees would be complete without bringing up your obligations to your favorite Uncle Sam. As an employer, you'll be required to withhold several different types of taxes from your employees, including income tax, FICA (aka Social Security), and Medicare. You're also required to keep detailed records about the amount withheld and when it was sent in to the IRS (usually quarterly). Your accountant can help you set up a system for paying federal, state, and local taxes in a timely fashion and recording these tax payments properly. For more information about withholding and taxes, pick up a copy of *IRS Publication 15, Employer's Tax Guide,* as well as *Publication 583, Starting a Business and Keeping Records.* Both are available online from www.irs.gov or at your local IRS office.

And that's not all. The employer incurs a tax liability for every employee. You must pay the matching portion of the FICA tax, which, as of 2007, is 6.2 percent, and the matching portion of Medicare taxes (as of 2007 it is 1.45 percent). You also must pay state unemployment taxes (to fund payments to employees who are fired or laid off), a self-employment tax (that's the Social Security tax on your personal earnings since you're self-employed), and Federal Unemployment Tax (FUTA), which pays for unemployment insurance programs (another 6.2 percent on the first $7,000 earned by

Pump 'Em Up

Whether you have a two-person shop or one with a dozen or more employees, one of your most important duties as team leader is to build employee morale. Human resources experts say that acknowledging and using employees' ideas is crucial for the success of a company, not only because it encourages employee contributions, but also because recognizing their worth makes them feel like an important part of the team. Other ways you can build team spirit include:

○ Expressing appreciation for a job well done (a simple "thank you" or a small token like a $5 gift certificate for a fast-food restaurant can work wonders)

○ Celebrating accomplishments, such as when a new employee learns a new skill, like using a power buffer

○ Allowing employees to borrow company equipment when it's not in use to detail their own cars (with the stipulation that it must be returned in the same condition as it went out)

○ Offering criticism constructively and privately—never in front of customers or other employees

○ Making a reasonable effort to keep jobs interesting

○ Promoting a family atmosphere by hosting enjoyable activities outside work, like a summer barbecue for your employees and their immediate family members

○ Sharing product samples with your employees

○ Providing ear and eye protection, as well as company shirts and hats, at no charge

each employee). Luckily, you may be eligible to claim a 5.4 percent credit on this amount if you paid state unemployment insurance. Consult with your accountant. Finally, workers' compensation insurance payments are mandatory in all states except Texas. They cover employees' medical expenses and disability benefits if they're injured on the job. The amount varies by state, so contact your state labor department for guidance on how much to set aside.

With all these taxes, it's no wonder some small-business owners pay employees (or themselves) under the table instead of giving Uncle Sam his due. But don't do it. You could find yourself in federal hot water if you're not square with the IRS. And don't think no one will find out that you're not paying taxes. All it takes is one disgruntled

Interview Questions for a Detailing Technician

1. Where did you/do you go to school? _____
_____

2. What's your favorite subject? Why? _____
_____

3. When did you graduate? _____
_____

4. Where did you work previously? _____
_____
_____

5. Do you have any references? May I call them? _____
_____
_____

6. Do you know what an auto detailer does? (An important question—
a lot of people seem to think detailing is the same as customizing.)
_____
_____

7. Why do you want to be an auto detailer? _____
_____
_____

8. Have you done any detailing either professionally or on your own
or a friend's car? _____
_____

9. What do you think is the most important trait a detailer should have
besides the ability to do the job? _____
_____

10. Are you good with people? What makes you think so? _____
_____

11. What would you do if a client wasn't satisfied with a service you provided?
_____
_____

▲

customer, one jealous competitor, or even one angry ex-employee to bring the whole house of cars down on your head.

Another way some employers try to evade all this federal folderol is by using independent contractors rather than employees. An independent contractor is a person who's not actually on the payroll even though he or she provides certain services for your business. The problem is, this can be a minefield of potential problems because the IRS has very strict definitions about what constitutes an employee vs. an independent contractor.

If you're seriously interested in using independent contractors and want to stay on the right side of the law, visit the IRS site to download *Publication 15-A, Employers' Supplemental Tax Guide*, or pick up a copy from your nearest IRS field office.

You're Hired

Hiring someone is always both joyful and nerve-wracking. On one hand, it means you are growing your business, while on the other hand it can mean potential headaches, since you are now responsible for someone else. To ease your burden, you need to remember a few simple rules about being the boss.

- *Listen.* Sure it's easy to talk and to tell people what they need to do and how they need to do it. But you also need to hear their questions, concerns, and even an occasional good idea. And, if you do not like their ideas…

- *Criticize the idea, not the person.* Separate detailing and that which pertains to work from the individual, and never criticize or demean your employee(s) on a personal level.

- *Be human.* There are plenty of computer programs that can feed information to us, so we don't need to have humans playing the role of computers. Get a feel for when someone is too tired, overworked, or if there are problems brewing. Have meetings with employees where you can discuss what is going on. Open up a line of communications and you'll find that you get better results.

- *Never abuse your power.* You are the boss, in charge of their work at your company.

> **Tip...**
>
> **Smart Tip**
> Know what not to ask in an interview. By law, you cannot ask certain questions when you conduct an interview, such as whether someone is single or married, or their sexual orientation. Do not ask someone's age. Do not ask if an applicant is planning to have children or not. Do not ask if someone has been divorced. You see where this is going: Don't ask personal questions other than whether or not they are over 18 and a legal citizen of the United States, and you'll be okay.

You have the right to expect employees to be alert, responsible, competent, drug and alcohol free, and honest and diligent about doing their jobs whenever they are on the clock. You do not have the right to make judgments about their personal relationships, home life, or activities outside of your establishment. Being in power also does not mean you can ask for, or expect, non-work-related activities.

Stat Fact

Around 28 million Americans suffer some degree of hearing loss, according to OSHA, and noise-induced hearing loss is the second most reported occupational illness or injury.

- *People respond to positive reinforcement and incentives.* Gone are the days of driving an employee until he or she is at the brink of collapse. Most studies today show that positive reinforcement is the key to productive workers. If people feel that they are being treated well and are a part of the organization, they are more likely to do better work.

Rules and Policies

As frivolous lawsuits suck the breath out of many new businesses, the last thing you need is a disgruntled employee. To protect yourself, you should have your policies in writing. Create a short employee handbook outlining the basics rules of employment, including work hours, sick or personal days, vacation policy, and all other such policies that you wish to enact. Present specific grounds for termination, such as drug use or alcohol use on the premises, coming to work under the influence of drugs or alcohol, stealing, carrying an unlicensed weapon onto the property, or any lewd, rude or violent act toward another employee or a customer. Make sure to have a sexual harassment policy that describes how such matters will be handled; typically it is with an impartial arbitrator, since false claims can be damaging as well as legitimate ones. List specific procedures for opening and closing up the business and include how often an employee will be reviewed and eligible for a raise. Have each employee sign that he or she has read it. This way, should you need to dismiss someone, you have it in writing that they understood the policies when they were hired. It's not foolproof, but it can certainly help you in case of such legal action.

Workplace Safety Issues

As for government regulations, there's a whole government mandate devoted to workplace safety. The Occupational Safety and Health Act of 1970 (OSHA) has specific requirements that employers must meet to ensure the safety of their workers.

▲

These standards are very precise and deal with things like protecting your workers from injury when using hazardous chemicals (basically anything that can be inhaled), protecting them against noise-induced hearing loss, and providing proper ventilation when using flammable and combustible sprays (virtually anything in a spray can). You'll find additional information about OSHA regulations at OSHA's website at www.osha.gov. Beyond that, be sure to keep work areas free of items like used towels that people can trip over, and immediately clean up spills that can cause a slip-and-fall injury.

Owner's Manual: Your Guide to Professional Development

Since automotive detailing is an industry that requires such a high degree of technical ability and skill, you'd think there would be scores of educational and informational resources available to help detailers learn how to ply their craft in the most professional way possible. But surprisingly, that's not the case. There's no such thing as "Detailer

University," as R. L. "Bud" Abraham of Detail Plus Car Appearance Systems in Portland, Oregon, puts it, nor is there even a dedicated professional detailers' association. Instead, a lot of the education is provided by the chemical companies (which, of course, promote only their own products in their seminars); a few detailers or industry experts who have branched out into training; videotape training programs; and the occasional high school program that teaches detailing as an appropriate trade for young people who don't plan to go on to college. Perhaps because of this, a lot of the support in this business comes from the detailers themselves, who rise above the type of animosity that can be spawned among competitors in any profession and share their ideas and tips. Others like the anonymity of internet chat rooms, where they can wax poetic about products and grouse about problems.

There's a certain amount of frustration among detailers because of this lack of training and information, as evidenced by some of the posts on the detailing bulletin boards. But until someone comes up with the means and a plan to establish a new detailing association to replace the one that folded a few years ago, detailers are pretty much on their own.

This chapter covers the programs, publications, and other sources of information that exist to help detailing professionals do business better, learn new techniques, and grow their business. You'll find contact information for each resource discussed here, as well as many others, in the Appendix.

Industry Associations

While there are many organizations for everything from auto glass to petroleum, detailers have exactly one large-scale association: the International Carwash Association. Located in Chicago, this organization "serve(s) the needs of the carwash and detailing industry's professionals and represent(s) their interests," according to its website. The organization has been around for 50 years and has more than 3,000 members representing more than 18,000 carwash and detail shop operators. An annual membership is $225.

There are a number of regional carwash associations. You'll find contact information for the larger ones in the Appendix. For a more comprehensive list, visit the International Carwash Association website at www.carcarecentral.com.

Industry Publications

To stay current on news, information, events, and trends in the detailing industry, you should subscribe to publications that serve both the business owner and his/her clientele. Here's a brief rundown on some of the major publications:

- *Auto Laundry News* covers issues of importance to both carwash owners and detailers. Recent stories of interest to detailers focused on special detailing problems and their solutions as well as detailing the engine compartment. One year, or thirteen issues, including the annual buyer's guide, cost $72. The annual directory alone is $15. Published by E.W. Williams Publications Co. (www.carwashmag.com)

Dollar Stretcher

The cost of professional publications is deductible on your business income taxes. A copy of your cancelled check when ordering a subscription, or an invoice paid in full is sufficient proof of purchase for the IRS.

- *Auto Trim & Restyling News* provides updates on current news and new product information, plus sales techniques to help your business attract more customers. For 11 issues, plus a free annual *Product Source Directory*, you pay $19.95. (www.atrn.com)

- *Auto Week*, which calls itself America's fastest car magazine, is a weekly consumer magazine that covers vehicle tests, industry news, race coverage, and other cool auto news. A one-year subscription (51 issues) costs $29.95. Published by Crain Communications. (www.autoweek.com)

- *Detailer's Digest* costs $15 for six tabloid-sized issues. It's published monthly by *Mobile Tech News* at www.mobile-technews.com. You'll also find *Mobile Tech News* on the same site.

- *Modern Car Care* is a national trade magazine for the car-care industry that covers business issues of interest to carwash, detail shop, and fast lube operators. A one-year subscription costs $47, or $60 in Canada. The MCC FactBook 2007 costs $20, or $30 in Canada. Published by Virgo Publishing Inc. (www.moderncarcare.com)

- *Motor Trend* (www.motortrend.com) is a consumer publication that includes reviews of domestic and foreign cars, comparison tests, race coverage, and new car previews—in short, anything the autophile needs to know. A one-year subscription costs $10. A Primedia Business publication.

- *Professional Carwashing & Detailing* covers the vehicle cleaning and detailing industries and their suppliers, with an emphasis on carwash issues. However, detailers will find enough between the covers to make the subscription worthwhile. Twelve monthly issues, plus an extra issue in November, cost $59. You can sign up for a free trial subscription at www.carwash.com.

Along with these industry publications, you can also find e-zines, websites, and chat rooms dedicated to Auto Detailing (see Appendix).

▲

Yearning for Learning

As mentioned previously, there aren't many formal training programs available to aspiring detailers. At Penn Foster Career School (pennfoster.edu), you can take home courses on auto detailing in the Career School Auto Detailer Program. You can get trained in working on materials like vinyl, plastic, leather, and chrome as well as interior and exterior cleaning and using the detailing equipment and materials properly and safely.

Detail King (www.detailking.com) also offers detailer training. They have an Auto Detailing Marketing & Hands-On Training Seminar, which is held usually one weekend per month in Pittsburgh, PA. The seminar is limited to 20 students. Day one is an intense, information-rich detailers marketing class, day two is "hands-on" professional auto detail training class.

Perfect Auto Finish offers an affiliate program that is now being utilized by more than twenty detailing locations around the country. The affiliates train at Perfect Auto Finish for three to seven days and can then be invited to join the affiliate program for under $1,000 per year. Affiliates receive education, information, support, marketing ideas, data, product testing results, and equipment information .

Another educational option is the professional hands-on and instructional programs and seminars taught by industry professionals. One of the best-known programs is presented by Portland, Oregon-based Bud Abraham of Detail Plus Car Appearance Systems, whose five-day training program covers management, operation, marketing and advertising, merchandising and pricing, and sales strategies. The cost depends on the number of days and extent of the training and Detail Plus asks you to call them at 800-284-0123.

You can also get the benefit of Abraham's expertise at one of the detailing seminars he presents in major cities across the United States, which are produced in partnership with *Professional Carwashing & Detailing* magazine. Other fee-based training seminars are offered by Auto Detailing Institute (www.autodetailinginstitute.com), Rightlook. com, and Appearance Plus Inc (www.appearance-plus.com). You'll find contact information for all these companies in the Appendix.

> **Tip...**
>
> **Smart Tip**
> Annual industry conventions are a great place to network and trade tips with others who understand your business and concerns. Be sure to attend the social events as well as the business seminars for a chance to hobnob with other owners.

Certification

Alas, this is another area where there aren't many choices. However, the respected International

Carwash Association makes up for the lack by offering an express detail services certification as a way to validate your express detail services to your customers. The program comes on CD-ROM and can be completed in one hour, after which you take a certification test. Once you pass it successfully, you'll receive a certificate that can be displayed in your shop. The software can also be used to train your employees in the express detailing process.

> **Bright Idea**
>
> Home and garden shows are a great place to showcase your talents. Buy a car part from a junkyard, buff out half of it, then put it on display in your booth. You're bound to get a lot of comments and questions from attendees—not to mention requests for your business card and service brochure.

Product Seminars

Some of the best free training in this industry is sponsored by the chemical companies. Their motivation may seem self-serving (they want you to buy their products), but they actually are doing a good deed by inviting detailers to learn how to use the products properly. Check the websites of companies whose products you like to see whether they offer free training.

Trade Shows

Although most of the detailers that Entrepreneur spoke to didn't carve time out of their busy schedules to attend trade shows, these industry events (which are held at both the national and regional levels) can be very useful for a new detailing business owner. They usually include keynote speakers, educational sessions, and networking opportunities. ICA's Car Care World Expo is considered the industry's premier trade show for professionals, and the Midwest Carwash Association's Expo is one of the industry's largest regional car-care shows. These shows are listed in the Appendix.

On-the-Job Training

Along with reading some of the magazines, many detailers have learned their crafts working with those who are more experienced. Starting as an associate or assistant, or having a mentor, can be a wonderful way to soak in the tricks of the trade, and has been for many detailers. Much in the same way that numerous crafts have been handed down from one generation to the next, detailing is a skill, even an art, and many pros enjoy passing on their knowledge and training the up-and-comers who seem eager to learn. While the old pros may want to keep some secrets to themselves, finding someone who has been in the detailing business for years and working with them, even as an intern, is a great way to hone your skills.

Driving the
Competition

Are you the type of person who zaps TV commercials before the pitch person utters a single word, shakes subscription cards out of magazines and gleefully stomps on them, and uses the color advertising sections to wrap gifts when you run out of holiday paper? Well, those days are over, because now that you're gearing up to start your own business, you'll never look at advertising the same way again.

Advertising that's correctly targeted, and has a message that grabs attention, can be very effective for pulling potential customers into the orbit of your business planet. As Stephen Butler Leacock, a Canadian economist and humorist, put it, "Advertising is the science of arresting the human intelligence long enough to get money from it." As such, its goal is to make people aware of you when you set up shop, then keep them coming back as you become an established member of the business community. Here are some effective ways a detailer can arrest human intelligence.

Setting the Wheels in Motion

No doubt you'll be happy to know that you don't have to spend a lot to make a big advertising splash. Simple and cost-effective tools like sales letters, fliers, posters, newspaper ads, door hangers, and postcards are often all that's necessary to drum up new business. But you do need a flexible plan for marketing your services to your customers, because scattershot advertising is as bad as no advertising at all.

Your marketing plan does not have to be complicated. But it must be in writing, and it has to contain enough information to help you identify market trends and react to seasonal changes, since this helps you determine which types of advertising will be most cost effective. It should also be flexible so you can alter and update it as market conditions change. This helps you stay in touch with the needs of your customers and continually devise new ways to meet them.

The major components of a marketing plan are the following:

- *Executive summary.* This section summarizes the main points of the entire plan and should be written last, after you've hashed out your overall strategy. At most, the summary will be one page—at least, just a few paragraphs.
- *Objectives.* In this section, you'll discuss what you want to accomplish with your marketing efforts and create a reasonable timetable for achieving your objectives. Putting objectives into writing helps to solidify them in your mind and give you direction. Here are some sample objectives for a new detailer:
  - Earn $10,000 in the first quarter of operation.
  - Seek work from local dealerships to supplement regular business.
  - Learn how to perform new services the competition doesn't offer.
- *Market analysis.* You can use some of the information you included in your business plan for this section. Review the demographics of your market area, then make some assumptions about what types of marketing will work best. For instance, are you situated in a working-class neighborhood? Then coupons might work well. Or are there a lot of urban professionals in the area? Those prospects might respond better to a frequent-buyer program.

- *Marketing strategy.* You've got objectives on paper; now figure out what you have to do to accomplish them and include that info in this section. To illustrate, here's how you can turn the objectives given above into marketing strategies:
  - Earn $10,000 in the first quarter by detailing one car per day at $150 per car (six days a week = 78 days x $150 per car = $11,700).
  - Personally stop by each of the area's auto dealerships to meet the service manager and discuss the detailing services my company offers.
  - Take a course in paintless dent repair to attract customers that the competition doesn't service.
- *Proposed marketing activities.* This is basically a to-do list that includes all the marketing activities you're planning, like putting fliers on cars in the mall parking lot, the period in which you'll do it (pick the actual dates), and who will do the actual work (you, a high school kid you hire to slip fliers under windshield wipers, etc.). Try putting this information into a spreadsheet program like Excel or even on an accountant's pad so you can see exactly what you're planning and when it's supposed to happen.
- *Budget.* In this section, you'll make some assumptions about where you'll spend your dollars, like on those fliers mentioned above or door hangers (those coated paper tags that are hung on prospective customers' front doors).
- *Performance tracking.* Establish some benchmarks against which you can measure your marketing efforts. This helps you figure out whether your marketing strategy is working, what aspects should be repeated, and which parts of the marketing plan are not worthwhile. You'll find some additional information about writing marketing plans at the Small Business Association's website: www.sba.gov.

Did you notice that many of the items in your marketing plan are similar to those in your business plan? That's done deliberately. The difference is that your business plan gives the big picture, while your marketing plan is a more narrow view. Both are important to keeping the business on track as well as for obtaining financing. Lenders will be so impressed by your shrewd business sense and entrepreneurial spirit that they won't be able to write you that startup check fast enough.

Shifting into High Gear

Just when you thought you had done all the planning you could possibly stand, we have to break the news to you that you still have to plan your actual promotional strategy. First, set up a budget. A good rule of thumb is to set your budget as a percentage of projected gross sales. A budget of 2 to 5 percent is a modest, yet reasonable amount for a startup business.

So let's say you're projecting gross sales of $50,000 in your inaugural year. Using the 2 to 5 percent rule, that works out to an advertising budget of $1,000 to $2,500 a year. Luckily, most of the advertising tools that are most effective for detailers are pretty inexpensive—like a mere $45 for 500 fliers printed for 9 cents each at a local store such as Staples or around $375 for 2,500 postcards, plus postage. (If you're not going to use all 2,500 in a single mailing, make sure they're generic enough so you can use them for a subsequent mailing.) So even a modest advertising budget can go a long way.

As part of your startup costs, you should include a larger sum of cash for initial promotional and marketing costs. You'll want to make a grand splash to let your public know you're out there. Since advertising, marketing, and promotion can make or break a business, you should look at 10 percent (or even 15 percent) of your startup budget to put into advertising. Of course, if you are operating on a shoestring budget, you'll do what you can afford.

Reaching Your Target Audience

Advertising and marketing is most effective when you hone in on your target market. Therefore, you'll need to know which people, in which areas, are most likely to use your services. This comes from researching the areas just as you did when choosing a location. If you are a mobile detailer, this means knowing which areas you want to target and where you'll want to set up shop for a day or even a week, or more.

Once you know where you want to advertise, you'll need to determine which means of advertising is most cost effective. How can you reach the most people in that area, for a reasonable price? While the trick is to figure out which methods will work best in your market, the types of advertising that tend to work best for detailers in general are postcards, fliers, door hangers, newspaper ads, and Yellow Pages ads.

All of these will need to be carefully designed to:

1. Grab the reader's attention quickly, since most unsolicited mail gets tossed.

2. Highlight your business name, location and what sets you apart from the rest:

> **Bright Idea**
> Specialty items imprinted with your business name and phone number are an inexpensive way to advertise. Buy items that people will use, like pens, key chains, and even squeeze water bottles, then pass them around freely. Or leave them on the dashboard with a thank-you note after finishing the job.

your competitive edge may be a special skill, a lower price, more personalized attention, the latest in waxes and polishes, or whatever your specialty may be.

3. Make it easy for the potential customer to contact you to set up an appointment. Your phone number should be in bold print and your email address right there with it.

Be clever, try to create a graphically intriguing ad, but don't overdo it. A cluttered ad gets tossed. You can also draw people in with incentives, such as 10 percent off if you call by such and such a date, or have a friend bring in their car and get a special discount rate. Whatever you can use as an incentive, which might be a small freebie, can work.

Also, use the language that fits the market. Are these readers of *The New York Times* or of *USA Today?* Talk to your customers in a manner that will best reach them. Keep in mind that a variety of advertising and promotional methods are typically worthwhile. Also, regular advertising is more effective than a one shot ad. Yes, you may have a large newspaper ad for your grand opening, but otherwise, steady small ads in a newspaper or frequently handing out fliers (or having a student do it) keeps your name in the public's eye.

> **Bright Idea**
>
> You might have a modest grand opening event, which you'll also want to advertise. At this event (which might run from 11 a.m. to 2 p.m. on a Saturday), you could show off some of the vehicles you've meticulously detailed (offer a small honorarium to the owner—say, $50—for the privilege of displaying his or her vehicle), and provide snack food or serve something simple like hot dogs, potato chips, and soft drinks to induce people to stick around and look over the vehicles on display. Promote your grand opening and network with all who show up. Also, have something for the kids, even someone making balloon animals. Happy kids make happy parents—and potential customers.

Card 'Em

Postcards are an inexpensive way to reach a lot of people. They don't require an envelope, which is a positive because you can attract the recipient's attention quickly before they toss it. They also qualify for a reduced postage rate, and they can easily be created using the Postcard Wizard in Microsoft Word (among other software). All you do is type in the text, and the wizard does all the formatting. Just make sure the text on your promotional material is grammatically correct and error-free. You'll hurt your credibility as a careful and competent detailer by sending out a postcard that says you're "Noe open for business" or that you offer a discount to people who refer their "fiends." To save even more money, you can print postcards on your home computer, but by the time you factor in the time you'll spend feeding card stock through the auxiliary paper handler and the amount you'll spend on the materials, it

may actually be more cost-effective to have them printed for you. You'll find some printing resources in the Appendix.

As you'll recall from Chapter 3, you don't have to compile your own mailing list; you simply buy a targeted mailing list. Ask for the outputted list on pressure-sensitive labels, slap 'em on the cards while you're chilling out in front of the TV, and mail 'em. Then wait for the business to pour in.

"Advertising is good for generating high-volume work, like basic washing and waxing," says Prentice St. Clair, the San Diego detailer and industry expert. "It helps you appeal to a larger percentage of the population."

You can use postcards to announce your arrival in the business community, to introduce new services, to announce a sale on retail products you carry, and so on.

Paper Promotions

Speaking of advertising on the cheap, you can't beat fliers, advertising door hangers, posters, and brochures. Fliers are simple to create on your home computer. They're generally one-sided, on 8.5-by-11-inch paper, so they can be folded to fit a standard No. 10 envelope or tucked under a windshield wiper wherever cars are parked. You'll find a sample you can use for inspiration on page 122.

Although fliers are cheap, they, too, have to be professional looking and free of errors. "My partner and I made [our first] fliers on my kitchen table," says Anthony Orosco, owner of Ultimate Reflections in San Antonio. "They were horrible, and we didn't get one call from them. We invested some money in our next fliers, and the very afternoon we handed them out, we received a call from a business to detail a Lexus and two Mercedes. So let that be a lesson to all you aspiring detailing entrepreneurs: Don't skimp on your image! Go to the professionals for your business cards and fliers."

Often, the quickie printers like American Speedy Printing can help you design a nice flier at little expense. Alternatively, you can find a graphic designer in the Yellow Pages who will do the job for about $100.

Door hangers cost a little more, but can bring you a good look for the money. The standard size is 4 by 9 inches, and there's a hole cut at the top (known as a die cut) so they can be hung on every doorknob you can find. They're usually printed in full color on heavy paper that has a UV coating to prevent fading from the sun or inclement weather. One company we researched charges $444 (or 8.8 cents each) for

5,000 hangers. (This assumes that you use one of the company's templates; if you create a custom design, it will cost you more.) If you make the copy generic enough (for instance, avoid promoting a special sale or other dated event), the initial quantity will give you enough to blanket your target area several times. You'll find the names of a few companies that print door hangers in the Appendix under the "Printing Resources" heading. Before you go out and do the deed, however, check with the city you'll be working in to see whether a solicitor's license is needed to distribute door hangers. The cost is likely to be nominal ($10 or so), and having a license will keep you out of trouble in case one of the neighbors complains to the police.

Posters are a very inexpensive means of generating business. If permitted, you can post such materials on the boarding around construction sites, as well as in other businesses—offer to swap posters with another business owner to promote each other. Posters should include a photo or two of vehicles that you've detailed. Since the end result of detailing is visual, like an artist, you want your work to speak for you.

Brochures are useful for a variety of purposes. Format them to fit a No. 10 envelope, and you can use them for direct-mail advertising. You can also display them in a holder on your service counter (or hand them to your mobile customers) as a way to explain those lucrative add-on services you offer, like paintless dent repair, black trim recoating, leather treatment, and so on. You can also enclose them with a sales letter (see sample on page 116) sent to a selected mailing list with the intention that the prospect will read the letter when it arrives, then save the brochure for future reference. Brochures can also sit on the counter of a nearby auto parts store, and their brochures can sit in your waiting room. Barter with other non-competitive businesses. It's a great way to spread the word about your services.

Other paper ideas include menus. Talk to the owner of the local diner and see if he needs menus. Design something that fits the style of the restaurant and include a photo of one of your cars with contact information. Be creative and look for other ways in which you can promote your business on a steady basis.

Bringing In an Expert

To save money on the brochure design, you can use the Word brochure template. Just keep in mind that graphic design takes skill and creativity, and a do-it-yourself version might not project the image you're looking for. Consider hiring a professional to do the job. If that's beyond your budget, call the art department at your local community college or university and ask someone in the fine arts department to refer you to a talented student, who will charge you much less than a professional designer.

As for the copy, you might look for some help from a freelance copywriter. Often, he or she can improve upon your ideas and get the right wording. While it may cost a few bucks, professionals can make the difference between a mediocre brochure and something that will generate business.

Make your vehicle look showroom new again!

Spring special—Complete auto detailing just $175*

Price includes:

Hand wash and dry

Interior cleaning and reconditioning

(including carpets, upholstery, vinyl/leather)

Exterior buff and wax

Windows, tire/wheel cleaning, and more

Offer expires May 31

For an appointment, call

Great Lakes Automotive Detailing

5555 Jefferson Ave.

St. Clair Shores, Michigan 48051

(555) 555-0000

www.greatlakesdetailing.com

info@greatlakesdetailing.com

Pick up and delivery service available

Visa, MasterCard, and American Express accepted

*Average-sized vehicle. Price may vary depending on size/condition of vehicle.

Tricks of the Trade

Make sure your brochure includes your phone number, your brick-and-mortar address or post office box, and your website and/or e-mail address prominently. It's also a great idea to enclose a business card with any mailing piece that goes in an envelope because people are more apt to file a business card for future reference than a brochure. To get them to open the envelope in the first place, try some of these tricks used by direct-mail pros:

- Use only a return address (with no logo or business name) on the outer envelope to give it the appearance of personal correspondence.

- Use postage stamps rather than a bulk postage indicia, which is a dead giveaway that the envelope contains advertising material.

- Use a teaser line on the outside to induce the recipient to open the envelope. Teasers that incorporate the word "free" (as in "free estimate" or "Buy one service, get one free") or terms like "limited time offer" are powerful motivators. Of course, you then have to provide what you offer, or you'll be accused of false advertising.

Cooperative mail packages (aka marriage mail) like the Valpak also can be quite effective for detailers—if you're willing to offer a discount. They consist of numerous advertising fliers or coupons from a variety of different advertisers that are mailed to every residential and/or business address in a specific area. The fliers usually are sized to fit a No. 10 or a 9.5-by-5.5-inch envelope and may be printed in full color on glossy paper. The cost is usually quite low because your flier rides along with those from a lot of other paying customers. But the disadvantage is that your flier will be "bundled" with others from diverse companies like oil change companies, nail salons, window installers, dentists, and, possibly, other detailers. But the low cost may outweigh any perceived disadvantages.

A little while ago we mentioned that you should send a business card with every direct-mail piece you send out. But your card also can be used as a mini-advertising tool every day. Always keep some in a little holder on your reception desk if you have a facility or in your vehicle if you're mobile (just be sure to keep them clean and dry). Make sure to hand them out at all opportunities in which to network, such as local auto fairs or shows. You should also look into the possibility of putting a supply of your cards on the counters of companies that might be able to send business your way. Some obvious places include new- or used-car dealerships, quick-lube or express oil-change companies, bump shops, and auto supply stores. Obviously, you should check first to see whether any of them have their own in-house detailing shop.

Business cards are really cheap—so cheap it's not worth your time to do them on your home computer and printer. You'll pay only about $35 for 1,000 cards at national office supply stores like Office Max. If you hold any certifications from detailing

Sample Sales Letter

Dear Neighbor:

Before you know it, winter will be here again, along with frigid temperatures, overcast days, and nerve-wracking commutes home in the snow and ice. It's also the time of year that's the hardest on your vehicle. Road salt can eat away at your car, truck, or SUV, damaging its showroom finish, and dirt from the spray of slushy water can penetrate every crevice, from the wheel wells to the side-view mirrors.

Great Lakes Automotive Detailing can help protect your vehicle and minimize winter damage by prepping it for the rough weather ahead. In addition to washing your vehicle with meticulous care, we will hand-wax your car to give it the best possible protection against the elements. We'll make your interior look like new again. We can even remove tough odors and pet stains.

So before Old Man Winter makes an unwelcome return appearance, call the professionals at Great Lakes Automotive Detailing at (555) 555-0000, or visit our website at www.greatlakesdetailing.com. We'll put a shine on your car, truck, or SUV that will put that lazy old winter sun to shame.

Very truly yours,

Daniel Wayne

Daniel Wayne
Owner
Great Lakes Automotive Detailing

5555 Jefferson Ave. • St. Clair Shores, Michigan 48051 • (555) 555-0000
www.greatlakesdetailing.com • info@greatlakesdetailing.com

product manufacturers or chemical companies, you might want to include that information on your card because it gives you credibility.

The Power of the Press

Newspaper advertising can be an effective advertising medium for detailers, particularly when you're starting your business and need visibility fast. Community newspapers and free weekly shoppers offer the most value for your advertising buck, even though they're not published as often as the big city dailies. But even the weekly or monthly papers can pack quite an advertising punch because they're delivered right in the community where you do business. If the paper is free, so much the better, because that means advertising is footing the publication bill, and as a result, every single household will receive a copy.

Smart Tip

Before you spend your hard-earned cash on an advertising buy, request a media kit from the medium's ad representative. Media kits contain information that will help you decide whether the publication is right for you, including facts about its editorial content and readership demographics. It will also contain ad rates and an audited circulation statement.

Ads are sold in sizes as small as one-eighth of a page and cost less the more times you run them. (Running an ad just once or twice is a waste of your money—you have to be a regular advertiser to get the full benefit of your advertising dollars and for potential customers to become familiar with your company name.) For information about advertising rates and assistance with creating your ads, call the newspaper's advertising department. If you are creative and would like to design the ad yourself, you can use desktop publishing software like Microsoft Publisher to do the job. Make sure to include your contact number, address, and website and make sure the print is large enough so that it stands out. Many newspapers will simply ask you to forward them the copy and the graphic and they will lay it out for you at no extra charge. To get your creative juices racing, you'll find a sample newspaper ad on page 126.

If you specialize in detailing high-end vehicles, including high-performance and vintage automobiles, you might consider advertising in a city magazine. But beware: These types of publications tend to be expensive. A better place for your ad might be a regional collector car or car club publication. Check the internet to see what's out there.

Finally, a couple of really inexpensive advertising media are college newspapers and event programs (like those for student theatrical productions), as well as the backs of grocery store cash register receipts. Offer a coupon with a nominal discount, and watch your business grow.

You will also want to get a tear sheet, which is a copy of the page on which your ad ran. You do this for a couple of reasons. First, you want to make sure the ad ran

Sample Newspaper Ad

Make Your Wheels Look Like New Again!
Professional Auto Detailing

○ Cars/trucks/SUVs/vans

○ Hand wash/wax/buffing/polishing

○ Seat/upholstery cleaning/reconditioning/repair

○ Interior/exterior detail packages

○ Paintless dent repair/touch-up

○ Odor removal/deodorizing

○ Engine detailing

○ Same day service

○ Pick up and delivery available

○ Lease turn-in specialist

Great Lakes Automotive Detailing

(555) 555-0000
5555 Jefferson Avenue
St. Clair Shores, MI 48051
www.greatlakesdetailing.com

correctly. If it did not, and they made a mistake, you can ask them to make good on their error. You also want to save a copy of the ad, or advertising receipt for tax purposes, since this is a business expense.

When advertising in a newspaper, look through the paper beforehand and determine where you would want the ad to be placed. Placement is very important. Pages dedicated to fashion, reviews of the latest soap operas, or horoscopes may not be ideal locations for your ad. Sports pages, or any pages with auto- or vehicle-related services, are usually much better options. You can also try to coincide your ad to run with an upcoming car show or similar type of event. Inquire if they are doing a feature story or an upcoming review of anything auto related. Most newspapers don't have a long lead time, but they may ask for your ad copy two weeks in advance, so be prepared.

If you do choose to advertise in a local magazine, you will need more lead time, since most periodicals are put together at least one if not two or three months in advance. Again, inquire about anything that may be auto related in upcoming issues. You may also ask if they have advertorials. Some publications will include a short "article" on their advertisers. Since it's not actual editorial content, because it's featuring an advertiser, and it's not an ad, because it's written like an article, it is considered an advertorial. This short article can present some highlight of your business, what you specialize in, and how you got started. Some magazines will let you write it yourself, while most will have a writer call and interview you. Don't miss out if such

Bright Idea

Always test the potential effectiveness of your advertising so you are using your ad dollars wisely. First run your advertising idea by friends and other people whom you trust. They can give you objective feedback—for better or worse. Then, once you have an ad that you like, run the ad with a coupon in two newspapers but include a different identifying mark in each one. When customers bring in the coupons, you can count how many you got from each newspaper and know which ad brought in more customers. You may then decide to reword the ad for a specific paper (reaching a different audience) or if the results were poor, not run the ad in that paper.

an advertorial comes with the cost of advertising in the magazine.

All Booked Up

Anyone who has a business phone number automatically gets a basic line ad in the Yellow Pages, which gives your business name, address, and phone number. But the question is: Should you spring for one of the larger display ads (the ones that are boxed and sometimes have spot color) as a way to make your business stand out? To decide, open your local phone book and take a look at the "Automobile Detailing" listings. Are there many display ads?

"People who open the Yellow Pages have already made a decision to buy," says Barbara Koch, author of Profitable Yellow Pages (FTD Association). "But that's also what makes it unnecessary to buy a display ad in most cases. The real role of your ad is to get customers to choose you over someone else, and factors like your location may be what actually cause them to call you."

However, people have been looking in the Yellow Pages for decades and continue to do so, even with the internet available. Someone looking for an auto detailing place will notice the boxed ads much more quickly than the line ads and even think that this is a more successful company because of the ad. In short, Yellow Pages advertising has been very effective for businesses of all kinds for many years.

Ultimately, your decision to buy a display ad may be based strictly on cost. Display ads can cost a few thousand dollars and you're locked in for the year. The good news is that it's possible to include a lot of detail in the ad, like photographs and maps, but of course that drives the price up. It might be better to pay

Smart Tip

If your phone directory listing can accommodate your website or e-mail address along with your brick-and-mortar or mobile address, add the information, no matter the cost. A lot of people like to check a company's website before calling for an appointment, so put the information right up front to make it as easy as possible for them to find you.

for an extra line for your website address and let prospects browse your site instead of looking at a photo that will be too small to make much of a difference anyway. We'll talk about websites and other internet considerations in the next chapter.

Before we move on, here's one more reason you might want a display ad: According to a Yellow Pages Integrated Media Association usage study, three auto-related categories were among the top ten most-referenced headings in 2002, "Automobile Parts-New & Used," "Automobile Repairing & Service," and "Automobile Dealers-New & Used" had 561.1 million, 518.1 million, and 284.9 million hits, respectively. The used-car listings come right before the auto detailing listings in the SBC phone book, which means anyone looking at the new and used car listings might also see your ad.

Radio, Television, and the Internet

Radio advertising is not all that expensive. You need to consider which local stations have the right target audience. Ads are cheaper if they are not in drive time and if you buy in bulk you will get a lower rate. Make sure the ad is not too complex; something simple, clever, and inclusive of the name and phone number of your business (repeated at least a couple of times) can draw attention.

Television is more expensive than radio in most markets. Again, look for local stations or programs that cater to car enthusiasts. Again, buy in bulk. On television, you can showcase some of your work, so do so. Make sure your business name and location are prominent. While audiences may enjoy them, there's nothing worse for business than having one of those ads that is considered very clever or funny, but nobody knows what the ad is for. So, be clever but make sure your business stands out.

You don't want to stop advertising once business starts rolling in. Putting money back into advertising will help you draw new customers as well as remind those who

Radio Rewards

Dave Echnoz of 14/69 Carwash Supercenter in Fort Wayne, Indiana, has figured out the perfect way to get radio airtime without spending a fortune: He worked out a deal with a popular local station to get the DJs to do testimonials on the air. Here's how it works: The DJ casually works in references to the detailing business as part of the on-air chatter, as in "Hasn't the weather been terrible? My car really looks bad after all this snow, so I'm going to get it detailed over at 14/69 Carwash Supercenter this afternoon. They do a really great job." Echnoz says the testimonials don't sound like commercials, and best of all, he pays just $1,000 for 20 of these sound bites.

Beware!
Experts say that dissatisfied customers often won't say anything to a service provider when they have a bad experience, but they will tell six to seven people about it. Head off that kind of bad publicity by doing whatever it takes to make amends if you suspect a customer isn't happy. Good customer service is vital to your reputation.

have visited your shop before that it's time to come on back.

Internet ads can reach millions of people. However, that's meaningless unless you can do business on a very broad scale. Therefore, your goal is to be posted on local websites and in local online directories. Of course, you can always utilize your own website for advertising upcoming specials or newly added services. More on launching your own website later.

Make sure to ask callers where they saw you listed so that you can monitor all forms of advertising and determine which media is working best for your purposes. Many advertisers stay with a few primary means of advertising for a long time—as long as they are working. You can also make yourself available for television and radio talk shows, where you can serve as the "expert" and get free publicity by being interviewed or taking questions from callers. The same goes for newspapers and websites. Many websites and local newspapers are in constant need for content. Therefore, if you make yourself a columnist with a weekly auto detailing column, or even a blog, you can provide much needed content, while promoting your business.

Talking Up Your Talents

We can't conclude this discussion of advertising techniques without touching on the single most powerful form of advertising available—and one that's absolutely free of charge. We're talking, of course, about word-of-mouth (WOM). It's by far the best way to generate positive buzz about your detailing business, not only because it's cost-effective but also because other people do all the work for you. All you have to do is detail your little heart out in the most competent, professional way possible, and your satisfied customers will tell others about you.

You can also show them what you can do. Gary Kouba, former owner of Perfect Auto Finish in Roselle, Illinois, wanted to work on high-end cars when he started his business, so he scouted around and found the largest distributor of Lamborghinis, Ferraris, and Lotuses in the Midwest practically in his backyard—a "field of dreams of cars," as he puts it. Kouba offered to detail a car at no charge to show the dealer what he could do, and the dealer liked his work so much that he now delivers a car to the detailer in an enclosed trailer every other day—cars with sticker prices of up to $285,000. His predecessor, Kevin Traver, who owns the business today, also draws customers by running classes and seminars on car care. People learn what they can do at home, but they also see what the pros can do and some opt for a professional job.

There are other ways to generate positive WOM yourself. Try these techniques:

Stat Fact

According to a survey by Attard Communications, up to 54 percent of small businesses report they land most of their clients through networking, referrals, and word-of-mouth advertising.

- Call your clients shortly after completing the job to ask for feedback and verify that they're satisfied. Not only will they be shocked that you called (since it's very rare for businesspeople in service industries to follow up after the sale), but they'll be impressed that you cared enough to call—and they're likely to tell others about the experience.

- Leave a thank-you note and a small gift—say a bottle of vinyl dressing, a $5 gift certificate for the local coffee bar, or a long-stemmed rose—on the front seat where the customer will find it.

- Offer a referral reward to clients who refer their friends and family. The reward can be modest—say, 25 percent off a full detailing. Not only does this increase business, but also it makes salespeople out of your own customers.

- Donate time doing something positive and visible in your community. For example, you could hold a free detailing seminar for high school seniors who are interested in automotive-related trades. We'll tell you how to get free publicity for this type of event in Chapter 12.

- Go into chat rooms and onto online discussion boards and talk about detailing, mentioning that you do this professionally. You can add incentives for employees and customers to talk you up to a friend and bring in more business. There's also more you can do on your website, which will be discussed later.

Of course you can always put a sign on your dashboard or in your side window that says, "This car was detailed by..." then drive around town. Like Gary Kouba did, you can detail a couple of cars for free in exchange for having them also drive around town. Ask if you can park in a special place in or outside of a mall (which may cost something, but you can typically cut some kind of deal). People react to what they see around them. Razor scooters, for example, started out by giving scooters out to local kids who rode them around. Then other kids saw these scooters and wanted them, thus starting the scooter craze of the late 1990s. Likewise, one of the ways iPods got initial exposure was by people seeing the white headphones on commuters and asking what they were. Fashion shows at malls are ways in which clothing companies show off their wares, and sometimes they simply pay people to walk around wearing the latest styles. Seeing is believing and beneficial to your business.

Internet Marketing
and Research

Imagine having an enthusiastic, totally committed salesperson on your staff who labors for you night and day no matter what the weather, who isn't affected by the flu season, warm summer days, or high school football practice, and who doesn't ask for comp time. Well, you may already have Robo Employee on your staff. It's called the World Wide Web.

Along with finding a wealth of suppliers and the up-to-date info on new products related to the detailing business, plus chat rooms and discussion boards, the web is a great place from which to generate business. Posting on local web directories, advertising on other websites, and linking with similar businesses are all ways of drawing customers. Another way is by having your own site, which almost every business (and many individuals) now have.

In addition to easy accessibility for anyone on the web at any hour, there are many advantages to having a website. First, it gives you more visibility for very little cost. It allows you to post a comprehensive list of your services and prices so you and your staff can spend your time buffing and polishing rather than running though a litany of your offerings every time someone inquires about your services. It can be used to schedule appointments (if you have the right software) or automatically send out e-newsletters advertising specials and product sales to your valued customers or prospects.

For the purposes of this chapter, we'll assume you have at least a general knowledge of the internet, including knowing how to log on to an ISP, use a search engine, and send and retrieve e-mail. But if you haven't had much experience with this powerful medium, you should learn how to use it immediately. Virtually every community college and adult education program, and possibly your local public library, offers courses that can acquaint you with the basics of surfing the web. You can also tap almost anyone on the shoulder today and ask them to teach you the basics of being on the web, so sit down with a friend or family member and learn the basics.

Among the most familiar big name ISPs, you'll find: Adelphia, AT&T, Bell South, Cablevision, Comcast, Cox, EarthLink, MCI, SBC (which features Yahoo), Time Warner (which includes AOL), and Verizon. If you're constantly mobile, there are ISP services specifically for the laptop and notebook crowd, such as T-Mobile. For a solid review of ISPs you might look at Home Office Reports (www.homeofficereports.com) and see their ratings and rankings of the various service providers. For a much simpler chart, go to Consumer Search at www.consumersearch.com/www/internet/isp/index.html.

Also, ask other people which ISP they are using and how much they pay. You can set up the site under the host site. Those who are happy with their internet provider will generally let you know.

Your Own Cyber Space

The proliferation of websites over the first web decade has driven the cost of creating, hosting, and maintaining them way down to the point where anyone can afford them—even your niece in sixth grade, who probably has her own MySpace site. Many ISPs provide their subscribers with a certain amount of free web page space. This is sufficient if all you want to post is an electronic "business card," or a static site that doesn't allow navigation. This kind of site is useful for posting hours, telephone numbers, and other information customers might need when the shop isn't open. But to have a really great site, you have to be able to post useful information and change it periodically to give it a fresh, new look. That means you're going to have to pay for web page hosting.

Hosting Duties

To get your website up and running, you'll need a web hosting service. There are plenty and you'll find them by searching for web hosts online or by asking other small business owners who they recommend. After all, they are using services for their websites and you can get the latest on what they think of the service. This is how you can bring your site to the public through your website. To start, you'll need to select a unique name, known as a domain name (your web address or URL). Most detailers use their business name as their domain name if no one else is already using the name. (That could happen with a common name like "Bill's Auto Detailing," which would have a domain name of www.billsautodetailing.com).

Domain names are registered for a minimum of two years and are renewable. The cost to register a name for two years will typically range from $50 to $70. Of course you will need to do a domain name search prior to registering a domain name. One way to do this is by going to www.networksolutions.com, www.registerit.com, or www.domainit.com, and checking to see if your name choices are available.

Since so many domains are already being used, you should think up several versions of the name you want in case one or more have already been taken. Then search or check to see if the domain name you've chosen has already been taken. If it has, choose another. When you find a permutation that's available, register it online. You may also register some similar names if they are also available, such as both the .com and .net suffixes of the name, or common misspelling. For example, if, while trying to go to Google.com, you type www.gogle.com, www.gooogle.com or www.googel.com, you will still get www.google.com!

Of course, when thinking of a name today, it not only has to look and sound right, but it needs to be easy to spell and to

Smart Tip

If you want to sell detailing products online, you'll need a business hosting service rather than a standard web host. The premium price you'll pay covers the extra storage space as well as maintenance and upgrades on the site. It may not be worth it unless you foresee a lot of actual sales through the site.

Elements You Should Have on Your Website

1. **A homepage** that shows off one or more of your cars and provides your basic contact information in case someone just wants to call you. Also have a link to your menu of services.

2. **A summary page**. This page includes all of your services, packages, and your prices—and remember to update prices on your website should you change them. Most services make it easy to make such changes and they are typically not very costly.

3. **An "about us" page.** This lets people know who you are and puts a face behind the name. Give a short overview of your business, perhaps your mission statement and something about yourself. People like the personal touch and are not as easily drawn to faceless websites.

4. **Content.** You may not have much, but if there is something of interest such as tips or pointers for car enthusiasts, it will bring people back again and again. Along with short tidbits of information, you might have a Q&A section, testimonials from a few previous customers (don't make them up, it's illegal advertising), and/or a quiz, trivia contest, or something that is fun for your audience.

5. **A products page.** If you are selling products in addition to your services, offer them on a separate page where you can explain (in a sentence or two) what it is that you are selling.

Since it's more costly to set up an online shopping cart (unless you are selling a lot of items) you can have people order by phone or encourage them to come on in. Don't forget the photos of cars you have detailed.

remember. Also, for the sake of typing in a web address, don't make it too long. Nobody wants to type in the address www.fredseliteoneofakindcardetailingservice.com, (that's Fred's Elite One of a Kind Auto Detailing Service, whew!!). Instead you'd use www.fredsautodetailing.com.

Next you need a web hosting service to put your site on the map. You might check out the web hosting guide at www.hit-counter-download.com/web-hosting.html or at www.networksolutions.com. You can also do a search for web hosting services and see which ones you like. Asking for recommendations from other business owners is a very good idea.

What you want most is reliability (a service that is rarely ever "down"), a good monthly price (which could be anywhere from $15 to $100 depending on the number of pages, graphics, and your other needs), and good customer service.

When reading the descriptions and pricing, you'll find that some hosting services are clearly designed for larger scale business use and utilize a lot of features, hi-tech graphics, and so on. You need a relatively simple website with a few pages to highlight your business and possibly take an order—although a phone number and e-mail address should suffice, and save you money on your site maintenance.

Bring In a Pro Designer

Just as you hired a lawyer, and accountant and other pros, you should have a professional design your website. Have someone with experience design a simple website for you. This can be a pro designer or even someone knowledgeable in college who wants to earn a few bucks. A developer will do the programming work necessary to make your site look cool and make all the parts work together. Among other things, he/she will design the site's overall look, invent the flash intro, create links to lead viewers from one screen to the next (in essence creating a multi-page online brochure), and implement tools like site counters, if you want them. He/she also can set the site up so you can update it yourself or add new content easily.

A web developer will charge anywhere from $1,000 to $4,000 for a fully functional website with links. Part of this cost is based on the number of pages on the site. The more complex the site is, the more it costs. Future maintenance and/or updates are usually charged on an hourly basis if you're not doing them yourself. You can find web designers in the Yellow Pages or through your local chamber of commerce or other business organizations.

Gary Kouba of Perfect Auto Finish in Roselle, Illinois, hired a student studying information technology at the local junior college to design his website. The student created the site as an extra credit assignment, and Kouba paid him just $1,000 for what turned out to be a very professional job.

If you're computer-savvy, you could try creating your own web page by using one of the many web page programs on the market. Just make sure it is comparable to other professional looking websites. Here are some more website suggestions:

- Post your portfolio—or, better yet, a portion of it, meaning have a number of photos that people can look at of detailing jobs you have completed. Show some before and after photos to illustrate specifically what you did to the vehicle. "I see [my website] like an online professional portfolio that I can send to others so they can see my 'art,' " says Orosco, whose web address is www.ultimatereflections.com. "I see a car as a canvas, and the tools and products I use on it are my medium, so my website is a place where others can go and learn about who I am and what I do."

- Have a "forward to a friend" tab that allows the viewer to send an e-mail to his or her buddy letting them see a great detailing job or read your latest Top 5 Detailing Tips. People love lists, thanks, in part to David Letterman's Top 10

Lists. You might even have a great car related (tasteful) joke or a funny story that people can e-mail to their pals. This draws new people to your website, which should be posted with the e-mail that is forwarded to each friend.

- Showcase your work above the fold, which means place it where people will see it without having to scroll down. It should be clean enough to have a professional look, and don't pack tons of material on a page. Some white space is more professional than a cluttered web page.

Dollar Stretcher

If you decide to use a professional web designer to create your site, consider bartering for his/her services to keep the cost down. While it's unlikely you'll be able to barter for the entire cost of a $2,000 to $4,000 website, you could offer to give the designer a certain number of detailing services and a cash payment in exchange for the work.

- If you choose to use colors, make sure they are easy on the eyes and show up well on various computers. Remember, colors look different on different screens. For this reason it's best to go with light gray, blue, or other colors that won't glare in someone's face.

- Avoid anything that will slow the site down. Flash intros can be exciting and fun, but they can also lose people—or the viewer typically presses "skip intro." Most web users have already seen the "special web effects" and now want the meat and potatoes of the website, so proceed through elaborate intros with caution.

- Also, remember to update your website often. This will keep people coming back looking for new content, a new trivia question, and more importantly new special packages and prices. Stale websites give people the impression that the business isn't trying very hard.

- Finally, have your business name, contact information, and logo/slogan (if you have one) on every page.

Web Search Optimization

Web search optimization is a means of enhancing your chances of coming up higher on search engines. There are several means of going about this. One way is to pay Google, Yahoo!, or other search engines for higher priority listings. If you'd prefer hold onto your money for other advertising resources, you can optimize your site in several ways.

First, you want to include some content, since content is king in the world of search engines, and new fresh content is like throwing fresh meat in the shark pool—

it generates attention from the search engines. Keywords are the other main attraction and you need to include words and phrases that people might use to search for your business. For example, words and phrases like: buffed, waxed, auto, auto detailing, new car look, auto interior cleaning, and so on can all be worked into your content to enhance your chances of being located on searches. If you use your location, such as "Toledo detailing" or "Toledo auto detailing" as keywords, this can also be effective since people in the area will look up a topic (or seek out a business) along with a nearby location.

> **Smart Tip** Tip...
>
> Website type in colors like yellow can be very difficult to read against a light background. By the same token, don't use colors like royal blue on a black background. If you want your message to come through loud and clear, use black type on a white background. You can't go wrong.

Links, especially incoming, are also a plus in optimization circles. Therefore, if you can exchange links with other businesses (especially relevant ones), it will help you optimize your site. Look to exchange links with auto parts dealers, new and used car dealers, car washes, and other such businesses. Meta tags, the little two or three word descriptions that come up when you scroll across a highlighted link in the text, are also important, so make sure yours are included. Keep them simple.

Finally, try to keep the site clean, meaning dump any extraneous or slow loading material and don't tack on tons of pages. A few pages that load quickly and "give the people what they want" in terms of information about your business, plus fresh content, result in a very clean and easy-to-navigate site that can move up in the search optimization world.

Your photos don't have to be professional-quality, but they should be taken with, and uploaded from, a good digital camera. Try to take the photos in bright sun (although not at noon when the sun is directly overhead), and make sure they're clear and the subject is level. Don't use special effects—your detailing work should speak for itself.

You can pick up a good digital camera for less than $500. This includes USB cables that connect with your computer, and basic software to catalog your photos and improve your picture quality. Using your computer software, or special photo software programs, you can enhance your photos—but don't overdo it.

Online Discussions

One really easy way to get information about what's new and exciting in the industry—as well as to commiserate with other owners—is to log on to a detailing industry-related online discussion forum. We've listed just a few in the Appendix, but you'll find there are many more out there. You also can post bulletins on detailing message boards to find useful information, including leads to people selling used orbital sanders—or even an entire detail shop.

You'll also find many sites that offer help with the myriad issues that small-business owners, in general, face. One place to start is the Small Business Association (SBA) website at www.sba.gov, where you'll find plenty of information including business management tips and financing options. Related to the SBA's site is score.org, a small-business mentoring site that can connect you to a local Service Corps of Retired Executives (SCORE) office in your vicinity. At SCORE, you can find people who have been in a similar business, if not detailers themselves, who can provide some valuable insight. The best part is that it's free! Of course, you'll want to check out Entrepreneur magazine's website at www.entrepreneur.com for a wealth of comprehensive information on running a small business.

The best thing about the information you can gather on the internet is that much of it is available to you at no charge other than paying for your online cable or DSL service (dial up is a thing of the past). But beware: There are virtually no restrictions when it comes to posting on a website or a bulletin board message, so pick your sources carefully. When gathering information, or doing research, make sure you're on a reputable site and check to see if the information is current and current.

Still another invaluable function of the internet is its communication capabilities. You can order supplies in the dead of night, then stay in touch with suppliers to find out when the polishes and waxes will arrive. You can also develop your own e-mail address book, which will help you keep in touch with clients and suppliers.

Tooting Your
Own Horn

Successful entrepreneurs have to be masters at shameless self-promotion. Oh, you can buy advertising to spread the word about the great service you offer and the outstanding detailing skills you possess. But, as you know, advertising costs money—and that's something you may not have mountains of in the early days of your entrepreneurial venture.

So take a tip from experienced promoters and incorporate low- or no-cost marketing and public relations tools like news releases, newsletters, feature articles, networking, and public speaking engagements into your promotional mix. Here's a rundown of how each one can generate the positive publicity you need.

News Releases

News releases (aka press releases) are a means of generating articles or media stories about your business. They are stories you don't have to pay for. Sometimes the newspaper or magazine will use the actual press release for the story, but that is rare. Typically, they will use the "who, what, where, why, and when" that you provide (the basis for a news story) and write a short article based on that information. In other cases, a reporter will formulate a TV or radio story for your release. Web editors, for websites in need of content, will also be a great place to send your press releases.

The key is to circulate such releases in volume, since only a few will get picked up. The more you send, the more likely something will catch the attention of a newspaper, magazine, or web editor; or a TV or radio producer.

You might be surprised by exactly how much news you'll have to pass on to editors. You can write a release about opening your brand-new business, adding new services or product lines, and hiring employees. You can also write about your detail packages and seasonal specials. The problem, however, is that many of these are only news to you and those around your business (but you should send them around in occasional press releases anyway). The key, however, is having a story that has broad interest and/or is unique enough to grab the attention of the readership of the paper. Perhaps you detailed the car of someone famous (locally famous is fine) or you just detailed your first yacht. Perhaps you are running a special charity auction at your business or sponsoring a local car show. Maybe a car that you detailed won an award at a car show or was sold for some enormous amount of money. These are the kinds of stories that fill newspapers and that readers often find of interest. The news doesn't have to be earthshaking—just interesting to a general audience.

A news release is usually one page long and gives enough information to pique an editor's interest. When writing the release, answer the basic questions of who, what, where, when, why, and how, and be sure to provide contact information so the editor can reach you if necessary. You'll find a sample news release on page 141 that you can use as a guide. Please note that formatting elements like "For immediate release" are standard for new releases, so you'll want to use them on yours, too.

Basically a catchy headline and three paragraphs do the trick. The first paragraph should include the key facts of the specific story, making it sound enticing (but not using hype). The second paragraph provides the details behind the story, such as how

NEWS RELEASE

For immediate release

Date: September 4, 2007
Media contact: Daniel Wayne
Telephone: (555) 555-0000

GREAT LAKES AUTO FEATURES TWO-HOUR WINTER AUTO MAINTENANCE CLASS TO KEEP YOUR CAR LOOKING GOOD AND RUNNING WELL

Everyone wants their car to survive the winter, but few people know how to keep their cars looking good and running smoothly through snow, sleet, and rain. With that in mind the detailing specialists at Great Lakes Auto are offering a one-time only, two-hour class on Sunday October 10th at 11:00, at their business location on 455 Main Street in Great Lakes.

"We want people to know what they can do to prevent the elements from eating away at their car's finish and causing rust and other damage," explains Wayne, a detailer for 22 years, who will head the hands-on demonstration along with his staff. The free class will also include tips for keeping the engine running smoothly, tricks to starting up on those sub-zero mornings, and how to get those layers of ice and snow scraped off without taking the paint along with it. "Road salt can eat away at a car's finish, while dirt and slush can work their way into every crack and crevice, and leave a film on windows that can impair a driver's vision. "It's good to be prepared, because winter can be very rough on your car," adds Wayne, who looks forward to this inaugural class.

Great Lakes Auto has been in business for three years now and is run by Daniel Wayne along with his younger brothers Mike and John. Together they steam-clean seats, carpets, and mats; condition vinyl and leather surfaces; and apply protective dressings to wheels, tires, and other surfaces. They also clean engines, trunks, interiors, repair dents, and help car owners survive harsh Michigan winters. They were featured detailers on the local cable show Tool Time (WXYZ) and at the Traverse Auto Show this past April.

For more information about the Winter Auto Maintenance Class or about Great Lakes Auto detailing, call (555) 555-5000 or e-mail dw@greatlakesauto.com it came about and/or who was involved, if they are well known, etc. The last paragraph, also called a boilerplate, can be reused again and again. This is a short capsule description of your business that includes when it opened, what kind of detailing it does, and so on. It's not an ad, so don't write ad copy like "We give the best deals in town!" Instead, provide basic information about your business in paragraph form.

To get your press releases in the right hands, some research is in order. Find out which editors at the local newspapers you should send to and/or who at the local radio and television would be the appropriate people to receive your releases. Also look for applicable websites, especially ones that focus on what's going on in the community. Most media outlets today take e-mailed press releases. In this case, make sure all of the important information is concise and right upfront so it comes up in the e-mail preview window. They might not open your e-mail or scroll down—so grab their attention in the preview window and even with the headline, which should be on your subject line. The "from" line should be your company and not an individual's name, since they might not know who that person is, but will recognize the company name.

You don't have to be a journalist to write a release as long as your basic writing skills are sound. If you prefer, you can use a freelance public relations writer, who will charge $25 to $150 for a one-page news release. You can usually find freelance writers through the Yellow Pages, local professional advertising organizations, the chamber of commerce, and university journalism departments.

Newsletters

Newsletters are about the hottest little promotional gimmick around these days. Even though just about every businessperson, from duct cleaners to welders, is publishing a newsletter, they're still a good medium for spreading the word about your particular business niche. That's because they're easy to create, inexpensive to produce, and really effective for delivering targeted information right into the hands of your best prospects. Plus, consumers like to read them, probably because they tend to be short and to the point. That's important, given how busy people are and how short their attention spans can be. (Think 15-second sound bites and Xbox games.)

Informational newsletters tend to work best for auto detailing professionals. Such a newsletter might contain checklists ("Six Ways to Make Your Car Really Shine"), information about detailing products ("The Three Products You Should Never Use on Leather"), facts about how the weather can damage a vehicle's finish, and so on. Even though it might seem like you're giving away secrets, you're actually subtly selling your own services. You simply add a tag line to the end of each story that touts your expertise. For example, on the weather story, you could end with a line that says something like, "Great Lakes Auto Detailing can help your car weather a hard Michigan winter in prime condition. Call (555) 555-5000 for a no-obligation quote."

If you run specials or sales or if you want to try offering a coupon for a service, you can promote this in the newsletter as well.

In keeping with the trend toward short, quick reads, limit your newsletter to just two pages, that is, a single 8.5-by-11-inch sheet printed on the front and back. This size works great because it's inexpensive to produce; you can do it yourself on a photocopier at Staples or another local printing location, plus it can be mailed in a standard no. 10 business envelope. And don't think you have to mail a lot of newsletters frequently to make your point. Four issues a year timed with the seasons, like a "spring cleaning" issue or an autumn issue with winterizing tips, will work. Surround your content with some simple graphics and plenty of promotional material for your business.

Your newsletter is a great way to remind customers that they need to call for a detailing appointment, while giving you the opportunity to upsell, or suggest additional services your clients might be interested in.

Writing and Producing the Newsletter

Unless you have some writing experience, getting the words right can be the hardest part of doing a newsletter. The best way to get your message across effectively is to start each story with the most important information, followed by details that support your main point.

If you're not comfortable writing anything more complex than a grocery list or you've forgotten more grammar than you remember, you probably should hire a freelance writer to pen the newsletter for you. You can find a freelancer through local professional advertising organizations, the chamber of commerce, university journalism programs, and even the Yellow Pages. Depending on the experience of the writer, you can expect to pay $100 to $300 for a two-page newsletter. You might get a journalism student looking for some work for his or her portfolio. Even though they may do it for free, offering some money will make them work that much harder and the results will be that much better.

Also, remember that before you send anything out, proofread it very carefully.

E-mail Newsletters

Before sending out e-mail newsletters, you will need to establish a list of permission granted e-mail listings. That means you need permission to send to those e-mails or you'll be accused of spamming—which can destroy your reputation and result in your e-mail newsletter being deleted by spam filters.

The content is the same as it is on a printed newsletter. However, you can be interactive with an e-mail newsletter, conducting surveys, asking trivia questions or answering questions from your dedicated readers. Use this to establish some lines of communications with your customers and potential customers. Each time you e-mail

Free Publicity

The media are always looking for interesting stories to fill space on a page or on the air, and people are always interested in services. Keep your name out in front of the public as much as you can by trying some of these less-conventional promotional strategies:

○ **Become an expert.** Promote yourself as a local expert on all things related to vehicle maintenance and restoration by sending regular bulletins about detailing to the local media. Example: You just took a paintless dent repair course and the weather forecast calls for a freak hailstorm. Don't be shy—fax over a one-page news release to alert the media about how to handle hail damage. Include your business name and phone number prominently, and you could find yourself on the evening news. If you do get in front of the camera, make sure to get a copy of your performance—duplicate it—and have it ready in an edited version, to show your on-air talent for future endeavors. By the way, read up on how to act and dress in front of the camera. Hint, start by sitting up, NOT fidgeting, not playing with the microphone, and looking at the host of the program and perhaps (occasionally) at the camera. Also, wear clothes that are solid colors and not so bright that they will blind viewers or glare.

○ **Make a donation.** Donate a professional service—say, a full detailing—to your local public TV station for its annual auction. Or donate a tool (like a polisher) or a box of detailing products that can be auctioned. Anthony Orosco of Ultimate Reflections in San Antonio does this regularly and recently donated three full detailings, valued at $300 each, for an American Heart Association auction. "Every chance one gets to socialize and talk shop with potential clients gets your name out there even more, and then you will be known as an expert in your profession," he says. This isn't only a "TV thing" but there are plenty of community fundraisers in which you can participate.

○ **Support your community.** Donate materials or time to help a local environmental group or civic club. Your benevolence will resonate throughout the community.

○ **Take up a cause.** Actively supporting environmental protection can put you in the spotlight. But avoid controversial issues and politics. Whichever side you take, you'll alienate the people who support the other side.

○ **Sponsor a local sports team.** While this has a bit of a cost involved, it is a great way to put your name out there on the backs of the uniforms and/or on any local marketing or advertising done by the league.

a reply or thank them for filling out a survey, your name appears in their inbox and a personalized message from you—even a one line e-mail—can build a bond, one that will have them coming back again and again.

Make sure the page is not cluttered and that the content is near the top, so they need not scroll down to find it. Link your newsletter to and from your website—in fact, your site should provide some obvious places to sign up for the newsletter.

Bright Idea

If you're going after commercial business, like dealerships, create a pocket folder media kit for business prospects. Items in the kit may include a letter thanking the client for his/her interest, a service brochure or flier, copies of any articles written about the business, and information about you and your qualifications.

Use the space at the bottom to promote to your heart's content. Also, remember to add "Forward to a Friend" next to your content (with info on how to sign up) so that more people can find out about your news and sign up. This is called viral marketing, which means customers help you get other customers.

Finally, make the newsletter from your business and not from a person's name, so that the recipient will recognize it in the "from line" and try to be consistent with your styles and design. Don't forget to have the legal clause protecting people's privacy, meaning you do not (under any circumstances) give out your newsletter e-mail list unless you explicitly let your subscribers know that you are doing so. Also, include an easy unsubscribe button. Make it very simple so that people who elect to come back a few months later (and they do) can do so. If you make them jump hoops to unsubscribe, they won't come back.

You might find that designing the newsletter is somewhat easier than writing the stories. There are a number of affordable desktop publishing software packages that come with newsletter templates. You just type in the headlines, paste in the copy, and voilà—the program does the copy fitting and formatting. One program you can try is Microsoft Publisher, which is bundled in the Microsoft Office package.

If you'd rather detail cars than design newsletters, you can hire a graphic designer to create a template for you in a software program like Microsoft Publisher. Then you can reuse that template each time you produce another newsletter. You'll pay around $300 or so (or $30 to $60 per hour) for a two-pager. Check the Yellow Pages under "Graphic Designers," contact an art school or ask other local businesses that have newsletters for suggestions when looking to find a designer.

You can make your newsletter design more exciting and interesting by adding artwork. If you're doing an e-newsletter, feel free to use photos of vehicles you've detailed. But avoid photographs if you're going to photocopy the newsletter—the reproduction quality will be terrible, and the newsletter won't look professional. Another option is clip art, which is very inexpensive and easy to use. An all-purpose clip art package includes auto art that you can use over and over. You can also use the clip art on other promotional materials you create, like fliers . A good clip art package to try is ClickArt 400,000 from Broderbund, which retails for $39.99 and features (you guessed it) 400,000 pieces of clip art. In addition, Microsoft Word comes with a small selection of clip art, and you can go online to select from a wider assortment of images.

Bright Idea

A sure-fire way to get good publicity—and new business—is by sharing your detailing know-how in do-it-yourself detail workshops. Gary Kouba of Perfect Auto Finish in Roseville, Illinois, does this regularly and reports he gets a lot of business from attendees who realize detailing is a lot of work and best left to the pros.

Feature Articles

If you have a flair for writing, you should consider writing feature stories as a way to increase your business's visibility. Newspapers (both the dailies and community papers) are always happy to look at articles that touch on subjects in which their readers might be interested. Stories popular with newspaper editors include informational articles and how-tos (how to apply wax, how to use a buffer). As with newsletters, you're not just giving away trade secrets by sharing your knowledge and insight with readers; you're positioning yourself as an authority in your field.

Prentice St. Clair, the San Diego detailer, has started a whole new career for himself writing articles for publications like Modern Car Care. He's published more than 90 articles on a wide variety of detailing and automotive reconditioning topics and is a regular contributor to two of the industry's leading trade publications. So go ahead—you can do it, too. Write articles giving tips for applying wax properly. Share stories about home detailing disasters and tell how they can be fixed or averted. Or report on a fleet of vehicles you detailed for the local millionaire. The possibilities are endless. Feature articles for newspapers usually run 600 to 1,000 words depending on the publication.

Again, proofread your work or ask someone you know and trust to look it over for a second opinion, and for proofreading purposes.

Submitting Your Manuscript

A manuscript can be submitted in one of three ways: by typing it on 8.5-by-11-inch white bond paper with one-inch margins on all sides, saving in text format on CD, or by e-mailing it (attach the file and paste the text into the e-mail in case the editor doesn't open attachments). The manuscript should be accompanied by a pitch letter that briefly tells what the article is about and why it would appeal to the readers of the publication. Always call the publication to find out the name of the editor so your letter can be addressed properly (just think how you feel receiving "Dear Occupant" mail), and be sure to provide contact information so the editor can reach you later. Call the editor a few days after you send the article to find out whether it was appropriate for his/her audience and what you can do in the future to increase your chances of being published.

Networking

As you know from Chapter 9, there are only a few organizations nationwide that cater to the needs of detailing professionals. When you find them, join them, then participate in their meetings and activities, because networking is a very good way to gain exposure for your venture and possibly drum up new business.

You'll also benefit from memberships in business organizations like your local chamber of commerce and the Rotary Club. Besides meeting the owners of both small and large businesses in your community—people who may themselves need a detailer in the future—you can exchange ideas for doing business better and possibly barter services (like trading a full-service detail for printing). The cost to join such organizations is usually nominal and is deductible as a business expense.

Public Speaking Engagements

Americans love their cars, so what better place to talk about your detailing expertise than at car clinics, car meets, and cruises? While some events might charge you a nominal fee to set up a booth, others may be free—and still others may actually pay you to be on hand.

The next time you hear about an event where lots of car lovers will congregate, find out what you can do to get a spot on the fairway, on the route, or on the panel. Then come prepared to talk about detailing in general and to answer specific questions from your adoring public. And be sure to slip in references to your own business whenever possible, as in "That's a great question, sir. At Great Lakes Automotive Detailing, we use a chamois to apply products because it's nonabrasive and lint-free."

Also, never underestimate the power of trade shows—even home and garden shows—

Smart Tip

When attending networking events sponsored by professional business organizations, circulate and meet as many people as possible since everyone is a potential trade/exchange/bartering partner. Just be sure to make notations on the backs of any business cards you receive so you'll remember later why the person might be a valuable contact in the future.

for drumming up new business. "I've done the Annapolis Boat Show, where 90,000 people walked past my booth," says Mike Myers of Gem Auto Appearance Center in Waldorf, Maryland. "Whenever I'd give out a card, I'd say, 'Take two, take more, because if you have your car or boat done, others will want theirs done, too.' One job will sell the next two jobs."

One last tip for making an impression at an industry or consumer event: Take along a supply of advertising specialty items, like pens imprinted with your business name and address, to give away to the people you meet. They're surprisingly inexpensive, and they tend to find their way into people's pockets or desk drawers, where they serve as a reminder that you're ready and willing to detail the heck out of their prized vehicles. A quick search of the internet showed that one company is offering 500 ballpoint pens personalized with your company name for about $297, whereas another sells 1,000 neon stick-up calendars for $270, which is just 27 cents each.

Calendars are another good giveaway item. Small pocket-sized calendars imprinted with your company name and address are a good choice because people tend to carry them around with them and pull them out for all to see. To find a supplier for give away items, check the "Advertising Specialties" listing in the phone book.

Financial Fit
and Finish

Now that you've worked your way through this owner's manual and figured out all the standard equipment you need to start detailing for a living, it's time for a final tune-up that will enable you to fuel up your finances so you can embark on the ride of your life.

As you know, money is the engine that makes every business run. But it's the management of that money that makes the business last. It's not enough to be the best detailer in the city of (fill in the blank). You also have to know how much money is going out so you know how much you have to bring in. You have to be able to project sales and adjust staffing accordingly. You have to contain costs so you can put aside enough to stay afloat when business is slow during the winter months or when inclement weather shuts you down. Above all, you need to have enough cash left over after expenses to make the installment payments on life's many obligations.

Fortunately, you don't have to be a financial genius or hold a business degree to do all this. With the help of an accounting software package, a good accountant, and tried-and-true accounting methods, you can keep your business on the road to profitability. But in addition to persistence, it will take serious financial backing or sufficient personal resources if you're planning a site-based operation as well as a keen interest in the state of your finances, whether you're building-bound or mobile. It also will take a certain amount of fortitude, because the startup period of any business is labor-intensive and difficult, and the early years can be very lean.

In this chapter, we present all the financial liabilities you'll encounter on the way to earning a living from your detailing business. Then it will be up to you to generate

Looks Good

If you're leasing your building, exterior work like snow removal and grass cutting should be included in your monthly lease payment. However, you cannot assume anything—make sure to read the lease agreement carefully and if these jobs are not included, ask for them to be added into the agreement. If, however, you bought the facility, then you are responsible for all the upkeep. While maintenance cuts into detailing time, it's a crucial part of operations because the appearance of your building and property are a reflection on the work you do. Interior upkeep, including emptying trash, sweeping and washing floors, and cleaning the bathroom should be the responsibility of every employee, although it probably will be necessary to assign someone to do each job so it actually gets done. Laundry should be everyone's responsibility, since an average-size shop probably will have to do a couple of loads of laundry daily to keep up with usage. In addition to loading up the machines, everyone should pitch in to fluff and fold.

Overall cleanliness is really important, especially in the restroom, according to Tom Schurmann, former owner of Masterfinish in Lakewood, Colorado. "I had people comment on how rare it is to go into an auto shop with a clean bathroom," he says. "If I won't go into the bathroom myself, I wouldn't expect someone else to, so our bathrooms were always spotless."

the income to offset those expenses and make a profit. So, ladies and gentlemen, start your engines, and let's get cranking.

Operating Income and Expenses

This snapshot of your prospective business may look positively terrifying when you start filling in the numbers. Every month, you will have more essential expenses than lug nuts on a convoy of 18-wheelers, and you may have to steel yourself against the shock it causes to your system. But it's critical to keep track of debits and credits so you always know where you stand.

Although you can have your accountant create an operating income/expenses (I&E) statement for you, you might want to try doing it yourself using the simple worksheet on page 154, or using an accounting package like QuickBooks. In the meantime, we've given you samples on pages 152 and 153 that show the operating income and expenses for two hypothetical detailing businesses. The first business, Details on Wheels, is a mobile business whose owner flies solo, while Executive Auto Restoration & Detail is a fixed-location business that supports two part-time employees in addition to the owner. We've estimated monthly costs for each to give you an idea of how much a new business might incur. Among these costs are the following.

Mortgage/Rent

If you're operating out of a facility, this will be one of your largest monthly expenditures. As with any other mortgage, your payments are due on the same day each month, and unless your mortgage is adjustable, the amount will always be the same. So all you have to do is plug this number into your I&E.

⚠ Beware!

To avoid problems if you're ever audited, keep a log of business calls, then compare it against your phone bill every month. The IRS usually requires written records for any expenses you deduct, and it will be much easier to figure which calls are legitimate business expenses if you have a log to refer back to.

Phone

Ever since the telecommunications industry was deregulated years ago, phone rates have gone wild as telephone companies duke it out for dominance. So you'll need to check with your local phone company to determine which number to plug into your I&E. Charges can vary widely. Voice mail is extra. Call waiting is included in many plans, but may be extra in your area, as is the case with caller ID for name and telephone number display. If given choices, these two features are important, while most others are not necessary.

Operating Income/Expenses

Here are sample operating income/expense statements for two hypothetical detailing companies that reflect typical operating costs for this industry. Details on Wheels is a one-person sole proprietorship while Executive Auto Restoration & Detail is a C corporation with one full-time employee (the owner), two part-time technicians, and a 3,000-square-foot detailing shop in a large metropolitan area. Use the worksheet provided on page 154 to project your own income and expenses.

Details on Wheels: Mobile Detailing Business

Projected monthly income		$5,900
Projected monthly expenses		
Mortgage/rent	0	
Phone (office and cell)	$140	
Utilities (water only)	$50	
Postage	$10	
Licenses	$20	
Owner's salary	$2,600	
Employee wages	0	
Benefits/taxes	0	
Advertising/promotion	$350	
Legal services	$100	
Accounting services	$150	
Merchant account	$30	
Supplies	$150	
Insurance	$125	
Transportation/maintenance	$150	
Subscriptions/dues	$50	
Loan repayment	$360	
Online services	$40	
Miscellaneous	$300	
TOTAL EXPENSES	$4,675	
Projected Income/Expense Total		$1,225

Executive Auto Restoration & Detail:
Full Service 3-Bay Facility

Projected monthly income		*$15,100*
Projected monthly expenses		
Mortgage/rent	$2,000	
Phone (office and cell)	$200	
Utilities (water only)	$100	
Postage	$25	
Licenses	$20	
Owner's salary	$4,167	
Employee wages	$2,550	
Benefits/taxes	$750	
Advertising/promotion	$950	
Legal services	$140	
Accounting services	$350	
Merchant account	$30	
Supplies	$200	
Insurance	$325	
Transportation/maintenance	$50	
Subscriptions/dues	$50	
Loan repayment	$630	
Online services	$40	
Miscellaneous	$700	
TOTAL EXPENSES	*$13,277*	
Projected Income/Expense Total		*$1,823*

▲

Operating Income/Expenses Worksheet

Projected monthly income $_____

Projected monthly expenses

Mortgage/rent $_____

Phone (office and cell) $_____

Utilities $_____

Postage $_____

Licenses $_____

Owner's salary $_____

Employee wages $_____

Benefits/taxes $_____

Advertising/promotion $_____

Legal services $_____

Accounting services $_____

Merchant account $_____

Supplies $_____

Insurance $_____

Transportation/maintenance $_____

Subscriptions/dues $_____

Loan repayment $_____

Online services $_____

Miscellaneous $_____

TOTAL EXPENSES $_____

Projected Income/Expense Total $_____

If you're doing business in a small to midsize market, you probably can start out with a single phone line in addition to your personal phone line. If you call a major metropolitan area home, it might be a good idea to have at least two business lines. The second line could also be used for your fax machine, but be sure to have voice mail on that line so callers won't ever get a busy signal. If you're mobile and handling the administrative duties out of a corner of your living room, you still should consider having a second business line. You don't want your two-year-old to win the race to pick up the family phone. Install that second line in a place where only you will answer it.

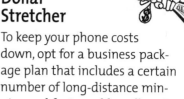

Dollar Stretcher

To keep your phone costs down, opt for a business package plan that includes a certain number of long-distance minutes and features like call waiting and caller ID. You can use your cell phone as your second line and especially on weekends when necessary, since weekend minutes are usually free.

Your cellular phone bill is also a legitimate business expense that can go on your I&E as long as it's used strictly for business.

Utilities

As mentioned in Chapter 7, site-based detailing shops need special plumbing to meet EPA regulations, plus they run a lot of powerful electrical equipment like generators, some of which may draw extra current. As a result, your utility bills may be high. To come up with a reliable estimate, check with your local city government offices to find out which utilities provide local services, then call their customer service departments and ask the representative to help you estimate your monthly bills. Be sure to mention what kind of work you do when you call (since you'll need more water than, say, a bookstore) as well as the square footage of your facility, so you'll get the most accurate estimates. For heating and power in general, you can save money (and help the environment) by using solar panels. After the initial expense, you can cut your heating and overall energy bills significantly on a monthly basis. Inquire by contacting a solar energy expert in your area or visit www.solarenergy.com for more information.

Postage

As mentioned in Chapter 10, you may want to do a mass mailing a few times a year to entice new prospects to use your services and remind current customers that you still appreciate them. First-class postage is an option, but you might be able to qualify for a reduced bulk rate. Just keep in mind that bulk mail is often perceived as junk mail, and the recipient may toss your carefully crafted advertising piece without even opening it. Also, if you anticipate having any monthly shipping charges (like for shipping retail products to customers), estimate and include those, too.

Licenses

It's quite likely you'll only need one type of license to open your doors: a business license that's renewable annually. You get it from the licensing department of the city in which you're based, and the cost varies by city. We're using $20 on our sample I&E just for simplicity's sake.

In addition, you'll need to buy renewable transport tags if you will be picking up and delivering dealership or customer vehicles. They're available from your state's department of motor vehicles or secretary of state, and although the cost can vary by state, you can expect to pay around $125 per tag.

Owner's Salary

Naturally, the salary you take from the business has to be figured in on the I&E to get a clear picture of the business's monthly expenses. Think carefully before you fill in this number on your I&E. Although you'll want to cover everyday expenses, you may find that making a few financial sacrifices now could benefit the business tremendously later.

However, Anthony Orosco of Ultimate Reflections in San Antonio recommends setting up a separate payroll account and paying yourself a regular salary even if the amount is irregular. "When you want to purchase something like a house or a car, you'll need to show a regular income," he says. "You may still have to show your tax returns for major purchases, but it looks better if you can show consistency in paying yourself."

Employee Wages

Wages will take a big bite out of your operating budget—possibly 30 to 40 percent of the cost of every vehicle you detail. You can keep your expenses down by keeping wages down, but you'll have unhappy employees who will think nothing of jumping ship as soon as a better offer comes along.

Prentice St. Clair of Detail in Progress in San Diego also pays a bonus on top of the hourly wage as a way to keep employees motivated. Tom Schurmann, former owner of Masterfinish in Lakewood, Colorado, preferred paying on a system known as piecework. "I pay my technicians 33 percent of the gross invoice with the understanding that the work had to be done right the first time," Schurmann says. "All work was quality-checked before the vehicle left the shop, and if anything had to be redone, it was done for free. That made employees pay more attention to the job they were doing."

For the sake of our hypothetical I&E operating expenses statement calculations, we've used the following wages:

Owner: $50,000 per year (salaried)

Two Technicians: Just over $9.00 an hour

Benefits/Taxes

Benefits are another expense that will cut deeply into your monthly income. For this reason, detailers often don't offer benefits other than perhaps a one-week paid vacation and the occasional sick day. Although benefits do make people happy, it's not always necessary to offer them. Tom Schurmann found that even when he offered to pay half the cost of health insurance, his employees didn't want a penny deducted from their paychecks. One of the reasons was because his technicians already had spouses with full-time jobs and full benefits. So he opted instead to pay a little more than the average for the piecework they did, and everyone seemed happy.

Figuring out the tax portion of the amount on the benefits/tax line is a little trickier. As we discussed in Chapter 8, there is a whole slew of taxes you'll have to pay on employees' wages, including the FICA tax, Federal Unemployment Tax and state unemployment tax, and workers' compensation insurance. Since you don't have previous records to compare to, you should estimate high so you're not caught short. Your accountant can help you make a reasonable guess.

Once you've calculated both the benefits and the tax figures, add them together, divide by 12 (for 12 months) and enter that figure on the benefits/tax line.

Advertising/Promotion

You'll want to estimate the cost of producing fliers, direct-mail pieces, newspaper advertising, and any other business awareness efforts you may decide to do. Yellow Pages advertising costs would also go here. Rather than trying to figure out to the penny how much you'll spend and painstakingly slot it into the appropriate month where it will be spent, get estimates on all the costs, add them up, divide by 12, and plop that figure in here. Don't skimp on advertising and promotion. Even if you are a superior detailer, you won't benefit if nobody knows you're open for business.

Legal Services

These fees can be a little difficult to estimate because you may not have regular monthly expenses. As mentioned in Chapter 5, some attorneys work on retainers, in which case you would include the whole amount of that cost on your startup expenses worksheet. If you use an attorney who works on a project basis, just guesstimate the number of hours you'll need his/her services, multiply that by the hourly rate, and include one-twelfth of that amount on your I&E. If you're going with a package of basic startup services and don't anticipate using the attorney much after that, include the entire amount on your startup worksheet and nothing on your I&E. You can always add a dollar figure into the "Miscellaneous" category later to cover any unexpected legal fees.

Accounting Services

While basic bookkeeping is pretty easy when you use QuickBooks or Peachtree, you should utilize the services of an accountant for the more complex accounting chores (including business taxes). Accountants are generally compensated on an hourly basis, so find out his/her rate, multiply that by a reasonable number of hours (say, ten hours a month), and use that figure on your I&E.

Merchant Account

Because detailing services tend to be pricey, it's unlikely that your clients will pay you with cold, hard cash (especially if you're detailing in the great outdoors). You can certainly accept checks or the occasional greenbacks, but you should also seriously consider establishing a merchant account that will allow you to accept credit and debit cards.

A merchant account is basically a clearinghouse for electronic payments. After swiping a credit or debit card through a point-of-sale (POS) terminal (discussed in detail in Chapter 6), you'll get an authorization code that tells you the customer's credit is good. The funds from that purchase eventually will find their way into your account, less a discount rate—which is a fixed percentage of anywhere from 1.5 to 4 percent per transaction—deducted from the purchase by the merchant account provider. There are other fees associated with merchant account maintenance, which typically include a statement fee of about $10 a month and a small fee for each transaction processed (usually around 20 cents). You also may have to pay a programming fee to get the whole shebang established, a monthly minimum fee, a "gateway" fee (for secure payments), a chargeback processing fee, etc. Since this is one industry that is pretty darned creative when it comes to fees, it pays to shop around for the best rates.

To get you started, we've provided contact information in the Appendix for several merchant account providers. In the meantime, we've optimistically marked down a merchant account fee of $30 per month on the sample I&E statements on pages 152 and 153.

Incidentally, if you're mobile, you'll have to go wireless to have a merchant account, which means you'll have your choice of really cool processing options and equipment. Wireless processing can now be done by cell phone or laptop, with a system known as AirPay Solution, with a two-way pager and a magnetic card reader, or with a wireless

Smart Tip

Before you can offer customers the convenience of paying with a major credit card, you must establish a merchant account through a bank or an independent sales organization (an organization that represents a bank or processor), after which you can buy a credit card imprinting device.

portable POS swipe terminal. One company that can hook you up with all these equipment and processing services is MerchantSeek, which can be found on the internet at www.merchantseek.com/mcommerce.htm.

Supplies

Since you're going to need a lot of different supplies for the business, you might want to separate the two main types of supplies. On one hand, you'll need assorted polishes, buffer pads, clay bars, towels, and all the other stuff discussed in Chapter 6; on the other, you'll need pens, legal pads, computer paper, and other supplies to run the business. For the expenses you don't incur every month, like business printing, just use the figure you got when you priced your business cards and divide it by 12 so you can come up with a monthly estimate that can be added to this amount. If you are going to also be selling a significant amount of do-it-yourself sprays, polishes, or other items, you'll need to add more to your "supply" category, since there will be an ongoing inventory.

Cash, Check, or Charge?

Since detailing is a big-ticket purchase, you'll have to offer your customers the option of using credit cards. So an important expense you'll incur monthly will be point-of-sale processing costs for accepting Visa, MasterCard, and other credit cards, as well as debit cards. The rates vary among the many merchant account services around. One company we found had a $10 per month statement fee, a 20-cents-per-transaction fee, and a discount of 1.5 percent (meaning you pay the merchant account company 1.5 percent of each transaction). Another company included free web hosting, a free business checking account, and other valuable services as part of its merchant account service. You'll want to shop around carefully for the best deal.

If you're planning to accept personal checks, a check verification service is also a good idea because it can reduce your risk of accepting a bad check. The cost is similar to that of a merchant account, and usually includes a discount fee on all checks you accept (rarely lower than 1.79 percent, according to MerchantSeek. com), a per-item transaction fee of 15 to 25 cents, and possibly a monthly minimum fee, a statement fee, and an application fee. But what you get is the best possible verification that every check you accept is good. Again, it pays to shop around for the best rates.

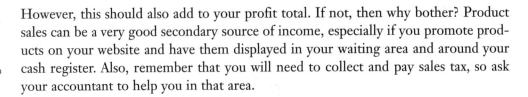
However, this should also add to your profit total. If not, then why bother? Product sales can be a very good secondary source of income, especially if you promote products on your website and have them displayed in your waiting area and around your cash register. Also, remember that you will need to collect and pay sales tax, so ask your accountant to help you in that area.

Insurance

Using the worksheet on page 60, tally up the amount of commercial garagekeeper's liability insurance you plan to carry, and divide that figure by 12 to come up with a number for this line. By the way, if you're using a personal vehicle like a van or SUV for your business that also doubles in off-hours as transportation for the family, you'll have to keep careful records about the percentage of time the vehicle is used strictly for business. Be sure to deduct those detours to pick up the kids from school during business hours or trips through the drive-thru window at McDonald's for dinner on your way home. The easiest way to keep track of these numbers is by keeping a simple mileage log. Office supply stores sell mileage logbooks that are small enough to stash in your glove compartment. Make sure you jot down business mileage every time you get behind the wheel, or your records won't be acceptable to the IRS.

Transportation/Maintenance

If you're mobile, keeping your truck or other vehicle in good working order is paramount since you'll be out of business if it's not reliable and ready to go when you are. Tally up the cost of regular tune-ups, then add in an amount to cover regular maintenance, like oil changes and spark plug replacement. Also add in the estimated cost of gasoline, windshield wiper fluid, and any travel-related costs, as well as vehicle payments if appropriate. We've estimated $150 per month for a mobile business since at some point you will pay that $400 parts and labor bill for something that needed repairing on a much utilized vehicle (factor that into your total and divide by 12). We estimated $50 a month for a detailer working from a standing facility who will put on a lot less mileage than a road warrior/mobile detailer. For mobile detailers, you might double this expense because the vehicle will be used much more.

Subscriptions/Dues

As discussed in Chapter 9, reading magazines and trade publications is a good way to stay current on issues of importance to detailers, so you'll probably want to subscribe to a few detailing and carwash publications. Don't forget to stock up the waiting area with car magazines as well as general interest publications like *People*, *Better Homes and Gardens*, and *Newsweek*. It would probably also be a good idea to put a few children's books out for the kiddies. Put them all in an attractive magazine stand in your waiting room, then add their cost (because this is a legitimate business expense) to your operating statement.

Among the types of membership dues you'll want to include here are the costs to join industry-related organizations and local business organizations like the chamber of commerce as well as any detailing associations, local and national.

Loan Repayment

Whether you borrowed money for a down payment on your building, for equipment, or for a vehicle loan, that figure has to go on your monthly expense report. This is also where you'd include any loans from family, friends, and investors (discussed later in the financing section).

Online Services

The average rate for dial-up services is $14.95 to $19.95 a month, although you can find bargain rates that are lower. A DSL or high-speed cable connection can cost $50 a month, while web hosting charges for 1,000MB of space can be as low as $9.95 per month.

Miscellaneous Expenses

This is a catch-all category for items like coffee for the waiting room, trash bags for collecting loose items left in a customer's vehicle, and cleaning supplies for the restroom. Adding roughly 5 or 6 percent of bottom-line total is usually sufficient to cover these miscellaneous expenses.

Receivables

Everything we've just talked about is the red ink on your balance sheet. Your receivables are what the black ink is made of. To help you get to that happy point when the black beats red (kind of like in rock-paper-scissors), use the accounting software of your choice so you'll always have a running total of where the business stands.

Forecasting Receivables

Here's a simple way to estimate how much money you'll need to earn to stay solvent and make a profit. Suppose your expenses are $13,000 per month and you can detail 3 cars per day at $175 each, you would then have $525 per day. If you are open on Saturdays, at 6 days, you would bring in $3,150 per week. Since a month has 4.3 weeks in it, that would bring you to $13,545. You would be just above breaking even. Using that as a base, you would want to look at the extras you can include. Suppose you add two paintless dent repairs per week at $150 each then you have a $300 profit. Add a few small extras onto your other jobs and perhaps you bring in another $100 pure profit. Now you have $400 at 4.3 weeks or another $1,720 in profits. The idea is to figure out what you need to break even and then start building upon that total. Considering the many possible offerings on your menu of services, you may need to spend more time crunching numbers to determine what you foresee as a realistic number per month for income—most of which (especially in the early years) you will be putting back into the business so you can continue to grow.

Collecting the Cash

Most detailers work on a cash or credit basis with payment due when the services are rendered. For this reason, you'll need to be able to generate a bill of sale or receipt when customers are ready to pay up. Programs like QuickBooks, among others, have a receipt template you can fill out to create a computer-generated bill when cashing out clients. If you're mobile, you should generate this receipt before you head out to a job or carry a small receipt book (available at any office supply store) that can be filled out when the customer pays.

If you work for dealerships or you have big-ticket customers like Waldorf, Maryland-based Gem Auto Appearance Center owner Mike Myers' boat customers, you may have to invoice them instead. We've included an invoice on page 163, plus you can find a template you can use in MS Excel. Be sure to bill regularly—monthly or biweekly—to make sure your cash flow is steady and so clients remember they had the service.

Bookkeeping Solutions

We've already alluded to accounting and business software several times in this chapter as affordable and user-friendly for many of your financial needs. Even if your last math class was in 12th grade, you can easily get the hang of the inner workings of one of these packages. One of the best reasons to rely on one of these programs for financial assistance is that it'll help you avoid inadvertent math errors that can throw your calculations off.

The most popular choice of the detailers we interviewed was QuickBooks Pro 2007 by Intuit for Windows, which retails for $209. Besides having an invoice template, it helps you track receivables, write checks, pay bills, and more. It also interfaces with Microsoft Word, Excel, and other software. Another plus, data from QuickBooks can be imported directly into income tax preparation packages like Turbo Tax. Even if you'd rather leave taxing matters to your accountant, you'll probably find that QuickBooks will interface with his or her tax software as well. You can find it at computer or electronics stores or from the QuickBooks website (www.quickbooks.com).

Invoice #32454

INVOICE

Sold to: Mr. Greg Jakub
5555 Allard
Grosse Pointe Woods, Michigan 48236

Description of services:

Interior Detailing
     Vacuuming, plastic and vinyl/leather
      cleaning, conditioning $29.95
     Deodorizing $25.00

Exterior Detailing
     Hand wash and dry, buff and wax $39.95
     Engine cleaning $49.95
     Tires dressed $15.00

TOTAL   *$159.85*

Thank you!

Daniel Wayne
Owner, Great Lakes Automotive Detailing

5555 Jefferson Ave. · St. Clair Shores, Michigan 48051 · (555) 555-0000
www.greatlakesdetailing.com · info@greatlakesdetailing.com

To be paid within 30 days of invoice date.

Another popular accounting package you might like to try is Peachtree Accounting. The Pro Accounting 2008 program retails for $169.99 and is available from computer or electronics stores and directly from Peachtree's website (www.peachtree.com).

Invoices

Always send invoices out promptly after completing the work—if you choose to have a specific day, such as invoices sent out every Wednesday, then collect them all for the week and send them out on Wednesdays. Make sure you keep your copies in a safe place where you can locate them. When payment comes in, note the date on which that invoice was paid in full or, if there is still money outstanding, keep those invoices in a separate file. Use invoice numbers for your own organizational and filing purposes as well as to specify which invoice you are referring to if you need to follow up with a client, customer, or vendor.

At the start of the month, look at where you stand regarding invoice payments. Who still owes you payment? You will need to notify them if payment is past due, and possibly send another invoice if you cannot reach the person by phone, e-mail, or fax.

Be diligent about getting your money, after all, you work hard for it. If all else fails, you may need to collect with the assistance of a collection agency.

The Cash Kings

Now that you have a pretty good picture of what it will cost to run your detailing business every month, you may also be painfully aware that you'll need some financial assistance to make your dream a reality, especially if you're going the facility route. The most logical source of funding is your friendly local bank, but you may find that they're not as friendly when you need to borrow money. They are often reluctant to deal with one-person and startup companies simply because such ventures don't have a lengthy track record of success.

To navigate your way around this problem, you'll have to shop around to find a bank that will welcome the opportunity to work with you. "Small-business owners usually do better by selecting a bank with a community banking philosophy," says Robert Sisson, vice president and commercial business manager of Citizens Bank in Sturgis, Michigan, and author of *Show Me the Money*. "These are the banks that support their communities and function almost as much like a consultant as a bank."

Bypass the big regional banks, and check out the smaller financial institutions instead, because they are more willing to accommodate small-business customers, according to Wendy Thomas, senior business consultant at the Michigan Small Business Development Center at the One Stop Capital Shop in Detroit. "Small banks

The Five Cs

All banks use certain factors to determine a business's creditworthiness. These criteria include:

○ *Collateral:* assets to secure the loan

○ *Capital:* owner's equity

○ *Conditions:* anything that affects the financial climate

○ *Character:* personal credit history

○ *Cash flow:* ability to support debts, expenses

are simply more willing to deal with small-business concerns and are more sensitive to issues like the need for longer accounts-receivable periods," Thomas says.

Alternatively, you could approach your local credit union for financing. Credit unions are nonprofit, cooperative financial institutions owned and run by their members and are generally more generous with rates, terms, and conditions. They may be more willing to assist you, but only if you're a member. Since there's a credit union for practically every organized group (including teachers, churches, military branches, and so on), it's likely you can find one in your area you can join.

Also, when you're at the bank or credit union, open a business checking account. You absolutely must keep your personal and business finances separate, even if you're a one-person business with a modest income.

Help from Uncle Sam

The U.S. government is actually pretty small-business friendly. For one, the SBA is devoted to small-business issues and resources. And, although the government defines a small business as any enterprise with fewer than 500 employees, it will be just as willing to help your one-person company as it would be to assist a whole chain of detailing superstores.

One way the SBA can be of particular assistance to you if you're planning to hit up a bank for financing is with its free counseling and training seminars on topics like business plan and marketing plan development. The SBA can provide you with tips and strategies you can use to make yourself and your fledgling company look more attractive to a bank. The SBA also offers a number of loan programs, if you want to bypass the banks completely, as well as counseling and training. They do not make the actual loans, but they can provide the guarantee you need for a loan. For more information, check the SBA's website at www.sba.gov or call the answer desk at (800) 8-ASK-SBA.

Get Your House in Order

Before going to any lending institution, you will want to get your own house in order, financially that is. While you are looking for a business loan, the reality is that the person behind the business is you. Therefore, it is you who will be putting up collateral and making the loan payments. A lending institution wants to know that you are a good risk; essentially, someone from whom they believe they will get their money back in a timely manner. Therefore, you will want to have an impressive credit rating, one that indicates that you pay your mortgage, credit card bills, and other payments on time. You can check your own credit scores with the three major credit report bureaus, Experian (www.experian.com), TransUnion (www.transunion.com), and Equifax (www.equifax.com). A score over 700 is very impressive, under 600 not so great. Prior to considering a business, you will want to get yourself out of debt and make sure you have no outstanding loans.

To make your case for a loan stronger, you will want to show your business plan to demonstrate that you have taken the time and effort to map out exactly what your plans are and when, you see profits. Make sure you have good, valid answers to support whatever you write in your business plan. Any "I don't knows" and you will seem unprepared to launch a business.

Additionally, lending institutions typically want to see that you are also taking on some personal risk. Therefore, if you need $35,000 to launch the business, and are putting in $10,000 of your own savings, they will see that you are also taking a risk. People who put in their own money are far more dedicated to making a business succeed than those who are not willing to take their own risk.

Shop around, just because one lender says no, another may very likely say yes.

Do-It-Yourself Financing

If you've always been a saver, or you're starting a mobile business (which generally has much lower startup costs than a site-based business), you may not need the assistance of the big lenders to get the appropriate startup funding. Sometimes personal savings are enough to pay for the basics, especially when supplemented with a small unsecured personal loan from a bank or credit union. Unsecured loans are much easier to obtain than business loans, assuming you have a good credit rating and a record of paying

Smart Tip

Banks use three measures to determine your business's ability to make a profit: the gross profit margin, the operating profit margin, and the net profit margin. The decision to lend is made based on this information because it's the best indication of whether you're a good financial risk.

your debts on time. If you decide to go this route, consider every source of personal capital you may have, including savings accounts and certificates of deposit; income tax refunds; stocks and bonds; savings bonds; real estate, vehicles, and personal assets like jewelry (all of which can be sold to raise cash). You also have retirement plans, but these are areas you should leave alone in case you are unable to keep on detailing in your senior years. Remember, you should never sink everything into any business venture. It's too great a risk.

If your personal savings just amount to a nest egg, you might consider using a home equity line of credit to cover initial costs—assuming your bank is willing to give you one for a business startup. Just be very aware that if the unthinkable happens and your business doesn't succeed, your home is the collateral and would be sold by the bank to recoup its money. If you don't have a high tolerance for stress, another source of financing might be more advisable.

Personal credit cards are yet another common source of startup cash, although you have to make sure you watch your expenses closely. You don't want to skimp on equipment and tools, but when you're using plastic, it's always tempting to buy stuff with all the bells and whistles when just the basics will do. Get the best you afford without spending big bucks so you do not start your business encumbered with a huge debt.

If all else fails, you could borrow money from friends and family, but of course that can be a sticky situation. Make sure to handle the transaction in a professional, businesslike way. Always sign a promissory note that details repayment terms and offers an equitable interest rate, then faithfully make payments on the loan just like you'd make payments on your car or mortgage. Be careful to make sure that from a business and emotional standpoint, money matters will not interfere with your relationship—there are too many stories of friends and family members fighting or parting ways over money. Hopefully, personal loans from friends and family will come at a better interest rate than those from a bank.

Angels and Outside Investors

Another option is to look for what is called an "angel" investor. These are wealthy individuals who invest in projects to make money. However, in many cases, they are retired or semi-retired, and are investing, in part, because of their interest in the subject matter. For example, those who sink money into a new theater production aren't always expecting to see a bundle of money in return. They

Bright Idea
To determine whether your local bank is small-business-friendly, review its annual reports for information about its financial focus and business outlook, the type of loans it makes to small companies, and the types of businesses it services, all of which are clues about the bank's commitment to the community.

do, however, enjoy the theater. Therefore, if you can find someone who is a wealthy car enthusiast, you might be able to get some backing from this individual. Perhaps a collector of antique cars might want to back you for a cut of the profits down the road. Typically, such investors are the result of looking around, networking, and seeking out a person or a few people who want to get in on the ground floor of a business they enjoy. The only real concern on your part (besides having your attorney draw up proper paperwork) is how much involvement the person wants to have in operating the business. While someone in this capacity may be a source of wisdom, if he or she is truly a detailer at heart—or formerly ran such a business—you don't want someone taking away from your goals, dreams, and ideas, so minimal involvement is typically your best scenario.

The Fast Lane
to Success

This is it—the final lap before you take the wheel of your own detailing business. It is our sincerest hope that the information you have read in this start–up manual will put you on the road to success and prosperity in your new profession. But even as we wish you well in your new venture, we would be remiss if we didn't point out one very sobering fact:

There is the distinct possibility that even with a solid foundation, sufficient funding, and boundless enthusiasm, your business may not succeed.

Business failure tends to occur among smaller firms because they're often under funded, poorly managed, or unprepared for economic downturns. But just remember: Henry Ford attempted and failed to start an automobile company several times before he succeeded with the Ford Motor Company.

So let's take a closer look at some reasons for business failure so you can figure out how to avoid being another unfavorable statistic.

> **Tip...**
>
> ## Smart Tip
>
> If you get into a cash–flow crunch, draft a plan to repay your creditors rather than just ignoring them until you have enough money to cover your debts. Most creditors will be willing to work with you because they stand more of a chance of getting their money back if you remain open than if you try to hide your cash flow problems.

Why Businesses Fail

Probably the number one reason for business failure is inadequate cash reserves. Obviously, it will take a while to establish your business and build a reputation, so you may find you don't have a lot of customers in the early days. Make sure you have a sufficient nest egg to keep the business running while covering your personal expenses. Depending on your comfort level, you may want to have a six–month cushion or maybe even enough funds for a year. These funds can come from personal savings, or they can be part of the start–up stake you get from a bank. No matter where it comes from, just make sure the money is readily available when you need it, even if you have to stash it in a low–interest savings account.

The SBA says that outside market conditions, including new competition or unexpected increases in the cost of doing business, also can contribute to business failure, as can tax problems, poor planning, and mismanagement. The SBA Online Women's Business Center adds these additional reasons for business failure:

- Over generalizing and trying to be everything for everyone, which can diminish quality
- Failure to define and understand your market, your customers, and your customers' buying habits
- Failure to price your products or services correctly
- Failure to anticipate cash flow adequately
- Failure to anticipate or react to competition, technology, or other changes in the marketplace
- Believing you can do everything yourself

Your Plan of Action

So how can you avoid these pitfalls and have the best chance at success in your new venture? Start by hiring professionals, like attorneys and accountants, to assist with business management chores. This is what they do best, and hiring them frees you up to do what you do best. We know it can be pretty hard to part with the cash to pay their fees in the early days of a new business, but it's truly worth it in the long run.

Make sure you keep a close watch on your finances and only spend on essentials for the business (which includes advertising and promotion). Knowing where your money is at all times will help you with cash flow and in monitoring your overall financial situation.

Knowing your market means understanding your customers and honing in on what they want. This means thinking from their mindset, not just your own. Stubbornness is at the root of many of the problems listed above. Be open to suggestions, listen to the needs of customers, and think ahead. By reading up on the latest trends in the industry, you can stay one step ahead of the competition. While you need not embrace every change that comes down the pike, you need to be aware of what is going on in the industry and in your community. If another detailer is opening up a shop down the road, you should know about it beforehand and be ready to do battle, or at least have a competitive edge that keeps customers on your turf.

Whenever possible, you also should learn as much as possible about business management techniques. Take a few courses at your local community college or university, or even through an adult education program. Just knowing the basics of finance, accounting, and marketing really can help you make better decisions that will keep you in business.

And finally, have a positive outlook. That might sound trite, but the fact is, entrepreneurs who are optimistic and have some chutzpah are often the most successful. Think of Donald Trump, who earned and lost a fortune, then earned it again; Ray Kroc, who took a humble hamburger and parlayed it into a fast–food empire; or Bill Gates, a self–professed nerd who founded an empire.

Is there anything these entrepreneurs–turned–billionaires would have done differently on their march to the top? Without a doubt. The same goes for detailers who have built successful careers out of nothing more than suds and solvents.

Anthony Orosco of Ultimate Reflections in San Antonio admits he should have shopped around for capital before starting his mobile business. "[Lack of capital] is the number–one reason why most detailers either fail or struggle," he says. "In the lean times, when work is slow or when you're [building] a client base, and you run out of money, it places a lot of pressure on the business, your marriage, and other personal and business relationships."

Waldorf, Maryland–based Mike Myers of Gem Auto Appearance Center (who started as a mobile detailer) wonders whether it might have been a better idea to stick with mobile detailing. "I probably was a much nicer guy [when I started out]," he says with a laugh. "Now I have two mortgages, a family, and a work family of six employees. I really enjoy detailing, but I don't do it much anymore. It always gave me a real sense of accomplishment—plus, no one could make a car look any better than I could."

Karen Duncan of Union Park Appearance Care Center in Wilmington, Delaware, would have instituted drug screening and driving record checks when she was in business for herself. "People present themselves well in an interview, then show their true colors after you've hired them. Checking these things would have cut out some mistakes," she says.

Dave Echnoz of 14/69 Carwash Supercenter in Fort Wayne, Indiana, encountered a lot of people who thought detailing was a humble profession not worthy of notice, and admits he shouldn't have let it bother him. "People used to shun me when they found out I managed a carwash and detail shop, and they still do, but of course I couldn't care less now," he says. "Even my own father didn't understand why I wanted to do this and used to try to get me to go to college. But when I built my second house—something he never had—he said to me, 'Dave, you've made it.' That was a great moment."

Bay Watch

Even though the detailers interviewed for this book all believed there were things they could have done better at the genesis of their careers, not one had any real regrets. Rather, they worked hard and relied on their own natural enthusiasm, creative thinking, and determination to get them through the lean years. As a result, they managed to beat the odds against small–business ownership and build careers that have been rewarding in both personal and financial terms.

They've also accumulated a truckload of experience on the trials and tribulations of what it takes to be a professional detailer. For example, there was the time that Mike Myers and two of his employees made the 90–minute trip to Baltimore's Inner Harbor to detail a boat. Upon arrival, they discovered no one had loaded the "laundry" (the buffing pads and towels they needed). So while his crew prepped the boat,

Myers went shopping and ended up buying "nice towels like you'd use at home," as he puts it, so they could get the job done. "Now we have a laminated checklist on the dashboard of our mobile unit that shows everything we need, and it's the driver's responsibility to go over it before leaving," Myers says.

Tony Orosco and his former partner, John Hernandez, learned the importance of pricing services properly when they did their first boat detailing. Because they had no idea what was involved, they seriously underbid the job; then, when they got to the marina, they discovered the boat was not dry–docked. They ended up cleaning and polishing the hull from a tiny rowboat. In addition to getting seriously sunburned, they had to go back a second day to finish the job—all for $125. "That was our first and last boat detail in the water," Orosco says.

San Diego–based Prentice St. Clair discovered that an incredible piece of business can come from just about anywhere. One day when he was detailing cars in an office park, he was approached by the personal assistant of a multibillionaire who needed a detailer. He ended up detailing in the man's 60–car subterranean garage, which, among other things, held one of every Jaguar ever built.

Since detailing tends to be a man's world, it's not uncommon to run into chauvinistic attitudes, as Karen Duncan of Union Park Appearance Care Center in Wilmington, Delaware, found out. When she first started in the industry, men didn't take her seriously. "I can talk about cars like the best of them, but they treated me like I was just a receptionist and would ask to speak to a man about their vehicle," she says. "That faded over the years as I developed relationships with customers, and now people even ask me to go with them when they're ready to buy a car. I don't charge them—I just like to do it."

Gary Kouba proved that persistence is key to finding new work. He once walked out of Walgreens and saw a red Ferrari parked in front of a dry cleaner. After tracking the owner to a nearby phone store, he promptly launched into a narrative of what he could do to fix the minor flaws he noticed on the car. The guy was sold, but he had Kouba detail his wife's BMW first. The customer was then so ecstatic about the quality of the work that Kouba was soon working on the Ferrari. "He has been one of my best customers ever since," he adds.

Your Formula for Success

It's easy to see that being an auto detailer takes hard work, persistence, and a sense of humor. Now it's time for you to take your place among the captains of industry. Good luck in your new business venture, and may you make every chassis classy!

Appendix
Automobile Detailing Resources

They say you can never be too rich or too thin. While these could be argued, we believe you can never have too many resources. Therefore, we present for your consideration a wealth of sources for you to check into, check out, and harness for your own personal information blitz. They are by no means the only sources out there, and they should not be taken as the Ultimate Answer. We have done our research, but businesses—like customers—tend to move, change, fold, and expand. As we have repeatedly stressed, do your homework. Get out and start investigating.

Associations

Canadian Carwash Association, 5-2325 Hurontario St, Ste 194, Mississauga, ON, L5A 4K4, (416) 239-0339, fax: (416) 239-1076, www.canadiancarwash.ca

Central States Carwash Association, 31 E. Berkley Dr., #200, Arlington Heights, IL 60004, (888) 545–9121, fax: (888) 545–9151, e-mail: CSCAcarwashpros@aol.com

Heartland Carwash Association, P.O. Box 932, Des Moines, IA 50304, (515) 965–3190, fax: (515) 965–3191, www.heartlandcarwash.org

International Carwash Association, 401 N. Michigan Ave., Chicago, IL 60611, (888) ICA–8422, e-mail: ica@sba.com, www.carcarecentral.com

Mid–Atlantic Carwash Association, The Acumen Group, 2900 Linden Ln., #120, Silver Spring, MD 20910, (310) 962–8000, fax: (301) 495–8870

Midwest Carwash Association, 3225 W. St. Joseph, Lansing, MI 48917, (800) 546–9222, (517) 321–0495, www.midwestcarwash.com

National Association for Professional Detailing & Reconditioning, www.detailersassociation.com

New England Carwash Association (NECA), c/o The Association Advantage, 591 North Avenue, #3, 2nd Fl., Wakefield, MA 01880, (781) 245-7400, fax: (781) 245-6487, www.newenglandcarwash.org

Southeastern Carwash Association, 638 Independence Parkway, Suite 100, Chesapeake, VA 23320, (800) 834-9706, fax: (757) 473-9897, www.secwa.org

Southwest Carwash Association, 4600 Spicewood Springs Rd., #103, Austin, TX 78759, (512) 343–9023, fax: (512) 343–1530, www.swcarwash.org

Western Carwash Association, 8119 Somerset Blvd., Paramount, CA 90723 (562) 633-9274, fax (562) 633-9555, www.wcwa.org

Auto Detailing Books

Automotive Detailing: A Complete Car Guide for Auto Enthusiasts and Detailing Professionals by Don Taylor, HP Trade, 1998

Garage and Workshop Gear Guide, by Tom Benford, Motorbooks, 2006

Ultimate Auto Detailing Projects by David H Jacobs Jr., Motorbooks, 2003

Ultimate Garage Handbook by Richard Newton, Motorbooks, 2004

Ultimate Garages by Phil Berg, Motorbooks, 2003

Credit Reports

Equifax Credit Information Services, Inc., P.O. Box 740241, Atlanta, GA 30374. Order credit report by phone: (800) 685-1111, www.equifax.com

Experian, order credit report by phone: (888) 397-3742, www.experian.com

Transunion, free annual credit report: (877) 322-8228, www.transunion.com

Demographic Information

Buy Demographics, (800) 504-1708, www.buydemographics.com

Demographics Now, www.demographicsnow.com

U.S. Census Bureau, www.census.gov

Detailing Franchises and Licensing Opportunities

Detail Plus Car Appearance Systems, P.O. Box 20755, Portland, OR 97294, (800) 284–0123, (503) 251–2955, fax: (503) 251–5975, e-mail: info@detailplus.com, www.detailplus.com

Dr. Vinyl, 821 NW Commerce, Lee's Summit, MO 64086, (800) 531–6600, (816) 525–6060, fax: (816) 525–6333, e-mail: tbuckley@drvinyl.com, www.drvinyl.com

FranchiseWorks.com, LLC, 345 N. York Rd. Suite C, Hatboro, PA 19040 (877) 824–4411, www.franchiseworks.com

Sparkle Auto, 163 Campus Drive, Garden City, KS 67846, (866)372-9559, fax (620)-272-0034, e-mail: info@aparkleauto.com, www.sparkleauto.com

Ziebart International Corp., 1290 E. Maple Rd., P.O. Box 1290, Troy, MI 48007–1290, (800) 877–1312, (248) 588–4100, fax: (248) 588–1444, e-mail: info@ziebart.com, www.ziebart.com

Detailing Systems

Appearance Plus Inc., 4590 Babcock St. NE, #106, Palm Bay, FL 32905, (800) 408–5020, (321) 952–3838, fax: (321) 952–4015, e-mail: info@appearance-plus.com, www.appearance-plus.com

Detail Plus Car Appearance Systems, P.O. Box 20755, Portland, OR 97294, (800) 284–0123, (503) 251–2955, fax: (503) 251–5975, e-mail: info@detailplus.com, www.detailplus.com

National Detail Systems Inc., 9452 Telephone Road, Suite 175, Ventura, CA 93004, (805) 647-0522, fax (805) 647-0082, www.nationaldetail.com

Rightlook.com Inc., 8969 Kenamar Drive, Suite 113, San Diego, CA 92121, (800) 883–3446, fax: (858) 271–4303, e-mail: sales@rightlook.com, www.rightlook.com

Education/Training Resources

Auto Detailing Institute, 340 Lower Mountain Dr., Effort, PA 18330, (888) 286-1935, fax: (732) 544-2142, e-mail: smiresearch@att.net, www.autodetailinginstitute.com.

Detail in Progress Inc., P.O. Box 6155, San Diego, CA 92166–0155, (619) 701–1100, fax: (619) 795–2993, e-mail: prentice@detailinprogress.com, www.detailinprogress.com

Detail King, 947A Old Frankstown Rd., Pittsburgh, PA 15239, (888) 347–0847, fax: (724)-325-4506, e-mail:support@detailking.com, www.detailking.com

Detail Plus Car Appearance Systems, P.O. Box 20755, Portland, OR 97294, (800) 284–0123, (503) 251–2955, fax: (503) 251–5975, e-mail: info@detailplus.com, www.detailplus.com

Kleen Car Auto Appearance, (201) 261-7497, fax (201) 634-0390, e-mail: kkleen@verizon.net, www.1car-detailing-training.com

Penn Foster Career School, 925 Oak Street, Scranton, PA 18515, (800) 275-4410, www.pennfoster.edu/category-automotive.html

Perfect Auto Finish, 630-947-2090, www.perfectautofinish.com. (Classes are held in the Chicago area.)

Rightlook.com Inc., 8969 Kenamar Drive, Suite 113, San Diego, CA 92121, (800) 883–3446, fax: (858) 271–4303, e-mail: sales@rightlook.com, www.rightlook.com

Ultimate Auto Detailing Technical Institute, 9600 Lorain Ave., Cleveland, OH 44102, (216) 939–2886, e-mail: detailsupplies@aol.com

Equipment and Supplies

303 Products Inc., P.O. Box 966, Palo Cedro, CA 96073, (530) 549–5617, fax: (530) 549–5577, e-mail: info@303products.com, www.303products.com

Auto Wax Co. Auto Wax Company, Inc., 1275 Round Table Drive Dallas, Texas 75247 (800) 826–0828, (214) 631–4000, fax: (214) 634–1342, e-mail: info@autowaxcompany.com, www.autowaxcompany.net

Car Brite, 1910 S. State Ave., Indianapolis, IN 46203, (800) 347–2439, (317) 788–9925, fax: (317) 788–9930, e-mail: info@carbrite.com, www.carbrite.com

Clay Magic, Auto Wax Co. Inc., 1275 Round Table Dr., Dallas, TX 75247, (800) 826–0828, (214) 631–4000, fax: (214) 634–1342, e-mail: info@autowaxcompany.com, www.claymagic.net

Chemical Guys MFG. CO., 3734 W. Century Blvd. #2, Inglewood, CA 90303, (310) 678-2838, (866) 822-3670, fax (309) 437-3542, www.chemicalguy.com

ClearKote, P.O. Box 1041, Eufaula, OK 74432, (888) 626–2727, www.clearkote.com

Detail City, 65 S. Houle Ave., Sarasota, FL 34232, (800) 541-4542, e-mail: customercity@detailcity.com, www.detailcity.com

Detail King, 535 E. Waterfront Dr., #7109, Homestead, PA 15120, (800) 939–6601, fax: (412) 462–9206, e-mail: support@detailking.com, www.detailking.com

Detail Plus Car Appearance Systems, P.O. Box 20755, Portland, OR 97294, (800) 284–0123, (503) 251–2955, fax: (503) 251–5975, e-mail: info@detailplus.com, www.detail–plus.com

Forever Black Car Care Products, P.O. Box 6909, Moraga, CA 94570–6909, e-mail: info@foreverblack.com, www.foreverblack.com

Lexol, e-mail: Carolyn@lexol.com, www.lexol.com

Meguiar's Inc., 17991 Mitchell S., Irvine, CA 92614, (800) 347–5700, www.meguiars.com

Pinnacle Car Care Products, (877) WAX–3100, e-mail: info@pinnacle.wax.com, www.pinnaclewax.com

Poorboy's World, (845) 627–5907, e-mail: poorboysworld@att.net, www.poorboysworld.com

PremiumAutoCare, The Perfect Shine, LLC, San Diego, CA 92024, (877) 855-3125, e-mail: sales@premiumautocare.net, www.premiumautocare.com

Professional Dispensing Systems, 883 Parfet St., Lakewood, CO 80215–5548, (888) 386–1247, (303) 238–8343, e-mail: info@pdsweb.net, www.pdsweb.net

Rightlook.com Inc., 8969 Kenamar Drive, Suite 113, San Diego, CA 92121, (800) 883–3446, fax: (858) 271–4303, e-mail: sales@rightlook.com, www.rightlook.com

Top of the Line Detailing Supplies, 110 NE Hwy. 45, Bonanza, AR 72916, (800) 533–5743, (479) 638–7302, www.topoftheline.com

Gift Cards and Gift Certificates

ecard Systems, 1-866-776-7409, www.ecardsystems.com

Gift Central, 537 New Britain Ave., Farmington, CT 06034, (800) 283–1695, fax: (800) 428–1951, e-mail: info@giftcentral.com, www.giftcentral.com

PaperDirect, 1025 E. Woodmen Rd., Colorado Springs, CO 80920, (800) 272–7377, (800) A–PAPERS, fax: (800) 443–2973, (719) 534–1741, e-mail: customerservice @paperdirect.com, www.paperdirect.com

SmartDraw, Easy certificate software (800) 817-4238, (858) 225-3370, fax (858) 225-3390, , e-mail: sales@smartdraw.com, www.ssmartdraw.com (You'll find numerous gift certificate and gift card printers and do-it-yourself software by searching the web.)

Incorporation Kits

Bradford Publishing Company, 1743 Wazee Street, Denver, CO 80202 (800) 446-2831, www.bradfordpublishing.com

Find Legal Forms.com, Pre-incorporation kits, (800) 959-5899, www.findlegalforms.com

Inc. Plan USA, Trolley Square, Ste. 26–C, Wilmington, DE 19806, (800) 462–4633, (302) 428–1200, fax: (302) 428–1274, www.incplan.net

Quality Books, 315 SW 50th Ave., Miami, FL 33134, (786) 552-5042, www.qualitybooks.com

Merchant Account Services

Merchant Accounts Express, 20 Trafalgar Square, Suite 466, Nashua, NH 03063, (888) 845-9457, (603) 262-1210, fax: (815) 550-1612, www.merchantexpress.com

MerchantSeek, www.merchantseek.com

Network Solutions Merchant Account, (800) 838-9699, www.merchantaccounts.networksolutions.com

Newsletters

www.autodetailingnetwork.com

www.autodetailingnews.com

www.autogeek.net

www.bettercarcare.com

www.detailcity.com

www.detailking.com

www.mobileworks.com

www.templatesforbusiness.us/word-news-auto_detailing.htm (Templates for your own auto newsletters.)

Office Equipment and Furniture

Bell Office Systems & Services, Inc., 222 Washington Street, Peekskill, NY 10566, (914) 737-3242, e-mail: sales@belloffice.com, www.belloffice.com

Best Buy, www.bestbuy.com

Machine-Solution.com, www.machine-solution.com

National Office Equipment Company, 13430 Damar Dr., Philadelphia, PA 19116, (215) 934-7500, fax (215) 934-5156, e-mail: sales@noec.net, www.nationalofficeequipment.com

Office Depot, www.officedepot.com

Office Furniture 2 Go, www.officefurniture2go.com

Office Furniture.com, www.officefurniture.com

Office Max, www.officemax.com

Paper Direct Internet, 1025 E. Woodmen Rd., Colorado Springs, CO 80920, (800) A–*PAPERS*, fax: (800) 443–2973 e-mail: customerservice@paperdirect.com, www.paperdirect.com

Staples, www.staples.com

Online Forums/Message Boards

Auto detailing, www.automotivedetailing.com /forum/htm

Auto Detailing Secrets of the Experts message board, www.web-cars.com/detail

Autopia, www.autopia.org

Detail City auto detail and car-care forum, www.detailcity.com

Detail Plus Car Appearance Systems, Ask the Expert: www.detailplus.com

Meguiar's Online discussion forum,www.meguiarsonline.com

Mobileworks Auto Detailing Forum, Car care forums, www.mobileworks.com

Professional Car Care Online, www.carwash.com

Rightlook.com, www.autodetailing.com/forum.htm (Reconditioning forums.)

Roadfly Forums, http://forums.roadfly.com/forums/detailing

Tintdude, www.tintdude.com/detailing.html

Point–of–Sale Equipment

Credit Card Processing Services, Bailiwick Office Campus, 252 Swamp Rd., Ste. 53–B, Doylestown, PA 18901–2465, (215) 489–7878, fax: (215) 489–7880, e-mail: Kevin@mcvisa.com, www.mcvisa.com

InfoMerchant Terminal Sales, to apply: (971) 223-5632, www.infomerchant.net

Merchant Accounts Express, 20 Trafalgar Square Suite 466, Nashua, NH 03063, (888) 845–9457, (603) 262-1210, fax: (815) 550-1612, www.merchantexpress.com

Point–of–Sale Software

Chargem, Capital Merchant Solutions Inc., 3005 Gill Street, Bloomington, IL 61704, (877) 495-2419, (309) 452-5990, fax (866) 313-0716, info@capital-merchant.com, www.chargem.com

▲

Credit Card Processing Services, Bailiwick Office Campus, 252 Swamp Rd., Ste. 53–B, Doylestown, PA 18901–2465, (215) 489–7878, fax: (215) 489–7880, e-mail: Kevin@mcvisa.com, www.mcvisa.com

Everest Software Inc., 21631 Ridgetop Circle, Suite 100 Dulles, VA 20166, (800) 382-0725, (703) 234-6600, fax: (703) 234-6680, www.everestsoftwareinc.com

ICVerify, (800) 666–5777, e-mail: support–icv@icverify.com, www.icverify.com

Merchant Accounts Express, 20 Trafalgar Square Suite, 466, Nashua, NH 03063, (888) 845–9457, (603) 262-1210, fax: (815) 550-1612, www.merchantexpress.com

PcCharge, GO Software Inc., 8001 Chatham Center Dr., Savannah, GA 31405, 1-877-659-8984, 1-912-527-4400, 1-912-527-4531, salesinfo@verifone.com, www.pccharge.com

Microsoft Dynamics, www.microsoft.com/smallbusiness/products/retail-software/point-of-sale

POSitive Software Company, 2290 Robertson Drive, Richland, WA 99354, (800) 735-6860, (509) 371-0600, fax (509) 375-0629, e-mail: sales@gopositive.com, www.gopositive.com

Printing Resources:
Brochures, Door Hangers, Fliers, and Postcards

ColorPrintingCentral, (800) 309-3291, www.colorprintingcentral.com

Printindustry.com, P.O. Box 2238, Ashburn, VA 20146–2238, (703) 631–4533, fax: (703) 729–2268, e-mail: info@printindustry.com, www.printindustry.com

Printing for Less, 100 PFL Way, Livingston, MT. 59047, (800) 930–6040, (406) 222–2689, e-mail: info@printingforless.com, www.printingforless.com

Print Quote USA, 23012B Oxford Pl., Boca Raton, FL 33433, (561) 451–2654, fax: (561) 725–0246, www.printquoteusa.com

Promotion Xpress, (888) 310–7769, e-mail: order@promotionxpress.com, www.promotionxpress.com

PSPrint, 2861 Mandela Pkwy., Oakland, CA 94608 and 177 Mikron Road, Bethlehem, PA 18020, (800) 511–2009, fax: (510) 444–5369, www.psprint.com.

Publications—Consumer

Automobile, P.O. Box 420206, Palm Coast, FL 32142–7446, www.automobilemag.com

Automotivedetailing.com, www.automotivedetailing.com (an e-zine)

AutoWeek, (888) 288–6954, e-mail: awsubs@crain.com, www.autoweek.com

Car & Driver, 2002 Hogback Road, Ann Arbor, Michigan 48105, (734) 971-3600, e-mail: editors@www.caranddriver.com, www.caranddriver.com

Motor Trend, 2900 Amber Lane, Corona, CA, 92882, (866) 542-2679, www.motortrend.com

PRIMEDIA Inc., 745 Fifth Avenue, New York, NY 10151, (212) 745-0100, fax (212) 745-0121, e-mail: information@primedia.com, www.primedia.com (Publishes several auto publications including: *5.0 Mustang & Super Fords, Car Craft, Chevy High Performance, Circle Track, Corvette Fever, GM High-Tech Performance, High Performance Pontiac, Hot Rod. Kit Car, Mopar Muscle, Muscle Mustangs & Fast Fords, Mustang & Fords, Mustang Monthly, Popular Hot Rodding, Rod & Custom, Stock Car Racing, Street Rodder, Super Chevy, Truck Trend*, and *Vette.*

Professional Car Care eNews: www.informz.net/ntp_cw/profile.asp

Road & Track, 1499 Monrovia Avenue, Newport Beach, California 92663, (949) 720-5300, www.roadandtrack.com

Publications—Detailing Business

America's Car Care Business, P.O. Box 25310, Scottsdale, AZ 85255–9998, (480) 585–0455, fax: (480) 585–0456, www.americascarcare.com

Auto Laundry News, EW Williams Publications Co., 2125 Center Ave., #305, Fort Lee, NJ 07024–5898, (201) 592–7007, fax: (201) 592–7171, www.carwashingmag.com

Auto Trim & Restyling, 3520 Challenger Street, Torrance, CA 90503, (310) 533-2400 fax: (310) 533-2504, www.atrn.com.

Detailers Digest, P.O. Box 5950, Clearwater, FL 33758–5950, (727) 531–7885, fax: (727) 531–7850, e-mail: DetailersDigest@aol.com

Mobile–Tech News & Views, www.carwashguys.com

Modern Car Care, Virgo Publishing Inc. 3300 N. Central Ave., Phoenix, AZ 85012, (480) 990–1101, ext. 1285, fax: (480) 990–0819, www.moderncarcare.com

Professional Carwashing & Detailing, National Trade Publications Inc., 13 Century Hill Dr., Latham, NY 12110–2197, (518) 783–1281, ext. 3167, fax: (518) 783–1386, www.carwash.com

Safety Equipment

Omark Safety, 3505 104th St., Des Moines, IA 50322, (515) 278–5422, fax: (515) 278–5702, e-mail: sales@omarksafety.com, www.omarksafety.com

Safety Glasses USA Inc., P.O. Box 1021, Three Rivers, MI 49093, (800) 870–6189, www.safetyglassesusa.com

Successful Automobile Detailers

Doyle, Rennie, Perfect Auto Finish, 1381 Ridgefield Circle, Carol Stream, IL, 60188, (630) 947-2090e-mail: ktraver@perfectautofinish.com, www.perfectautofinish.com

Duncan, Karen, Union Park Appearance Care Center, Wilmington, DE, e-mail: LovYour Car@aol.com.

Echnoz, Dave, 14/69 Carwash Supercenter, 714 Ave. of Autos, Fort Wayne, IN 46804, (260) 436–9274, fax: (260) 434–4990, e-mail: carwashsupercenter@hotmail.com, www.1469carwash.com

Myers, Mike, Gem Auto Appearance Center, 11750 Pika Dr., Waldorf, MD 20602, (301) 645–2415, fax: (310) 645–0412, e-mail: PolishYourBoat@aol.com

St. Clair, Prentice, Detail in Progress Inc., P.O. Box 6155, San Diego, CA 92166–0155, (619) 701–1100, fax: (619) 795–2993, e-mail: prentice@detailinprogress.com, www. detailinprogress.

Schurmann, Tom, Professional Detailing Systems, 883 Parfet St., Lakewood, CO 80215-5548, (303) 238–8343, (888) 386-1247, e-mail: info@pdsweb.net, www.pdsweb.net

Traver, Kevin, Perfect Auto Finish, (630) 947–2090, e-mail: Ktraver@PerfectAuto Finish.com, www.perfectautofinish.com

Trade Shows

Car Care World Expo, International Carwash Association, 401 N. Michigan Ave., Chicago, IL 60611, www.carcarecentral.com

Midwest Carwash Association Expo, Midwest Carwash Association, 3225 W. St. Joseph, Lansing, MI 48917, (800) 546–9222, (517) 321–0495, e-mail: midwestcarwash@aol.com, www.midwestcarwash.com

Mobile Tech Expo, P.O. Box 5950, Clearwater, FL 33758–5950, (727) 531–7885, fax: (727) 531–7850, e-mail: mobileexpo@aol.com, www.mobiletechexpo.com

SEMA Auto Show, Specialty Equipment Market Association, www.semashow.com, www.sema.org

Western Car Wash Association Annual Convention & Trade Show, Western Carwash Association, 8119 Somerset Blvd., Paramount, CA 90723, (562) 633-9274, fax: (562) 633-9555, www.wcwa.org.

U.S. Government Agencies and Business Associations

Internal Revenue Service (IRS), 111 Constitution Avenue, NW, Washington, DC 20224, (800) 829-4933, www.irs.gov

National Automotive Environmental Compliance Assistance Center, 1-888-grn-link, www.ccar-greenlink.org. (CCAR-GreenLink® is operated by the Coordinating Committee for Automotive Repair in cooperation with the U.S. Environmental Protection Agency. It is designed to provide information and assistance for detailers in regard to environmental laws and compliance. All of the documents are created by federal and state EPA and OSHA offices, as well as the automotive industry.)

National Association of Women Business Owners (NAWBO), 8405 Greensboro Drive, Suite #800, McLean, VA 22102, (800) 55-NAWBO, www.nawbo.org. NAWBO provides women business owner members with support, resources, and business information to help grow and prosper in their own businesses.

National Business Association, P.O. Box 700728, Dallas, Texas 75370, (800) 456-0440, www.nationalbusiness.org. This nonprofit association assists self-employed individuals and small business owners by using group buying power to provide health plans, educational opportunities, and other valuable services.

Small Business Administration (SBA), 409 3rd Street, S.W., Washington, DC 20416, (800) 827-5722, www.sba.gov. The U.S. Small Business Administration provides new entrepreneurs and existing business owners with financial, technical, and management resources to start, operate, and grow a business. To find the local SBA office in your region log onto www.sba.gov/regions/states.html.

Service Corps of Retired Executives (SCORE), 409 Third Street, S.W., 6th Floor, Washington, DC 20024, (800) 634-0245, www.score.org. SCORE is a nonprofit association in partnership with the Small Business Administration to provide aspiring entrepreneurs and business owners with free business counseling and mentoring programs. The association consists of more than 11,000 volunteer business councilors in 389 regional chapters located throughout the United States. They have helped over 7.2 million small businesses.

United States Chamber of Commerce, 1615 H Street, N.W., Washington, DC 20062-2000, (202) 659-6000, Customer Service: (800) 638-6582, www.uschamber.com. The U.S. Chamber of Commerce represents small businesses, corporations, and trade associations from coast to coast. Call 1-202-659-6000 or log onto their website to locate a regional branch.

United States Department of Labor – Office of Small Business Programs, Frances Perkins Building, 200 Constitution Avenue, NW, Washington, DC 20210, (866) 4-USA-DOL, www.dol.gov/osbp

United States Patent and Trademark Office, Commissioners of Patents and Trademarks, P.O. Box 9, Washington, DC 20231, (800) 786-9199, www.uspto.gov

Water Reclamation Systems

Rosedale Products, Inc., P.O. Box 1085, 3730 West Liberty Road, Ann Arbor, MI 48106, (800) 821-5373, (734) 665-8201, fax (734) 665-2214, e-mail: filters@rosedaleproducts.com, www.rosedaleproducts.com

Top of the Line Detailing Supplies, 110 NE Hwy. 45, Bonanza, AR 72916, (800) 533–5743, (479) 638–7302, www.topoftheline.com

Web Hosting/Domain Names

Apollo Hosting, 2303 Ranch Rd. 620 S., #135–301, Austin, TX 78734, (877) 525–HOST, (512) 261–1203, www.apollohosting.com

DOMAIN.com., (800) 583–3382, www.domain.com

EarthLink, (800) 201–8615, www.earthlink.net

iPowerWeb, 919 E. Jefferson St., Phoenix, AZ 85034, (888) 511–HOST, e-mail: sales@ipowerweb.com, www.ipowerweb.com

NetPass, Inc., 7075 Kingspointe Pkwy., Suite 9, Orlando, FL 32819 (407) 843-7277, (888) 296-7277, e-mail: sales@netpass.com, www.netpass.com

Webhosting.com, (888) WEBHOST, e-mail: sales@webhosting.com, www.webhosting.com

Yahoo!, (866) 781-9246, http://webhosting.yahoo.com

Glossary

Acid rain: rain that contains airborne contaminants and emissions (including sulfuric acid) from fossil fuel–burning plants, vehicles, and other sources that will etch vehicle paint finishes if not removed.

Air compressor: a device for powering pneumatic tools.

Black trim restoration: the process of restoring faded vinyl and rubber molding and trim.

Bonnet: used on an orbital polisher to remove cleaners, polish, wax, and other sealants.

Brake dust: the particles produced by a vehicle's brake pads as they rub against the rotor.

Brochure: a printed sales piece outlining your company's services and capabilities.

Carnauba wax: one of the hardest waxes available; works best when combined with other types of wax.

Carpet extractor: a device for pulling shampoo and rinse water out of carpet.

Cement removal: removal of cement particles or film from vehicle paint and trim.

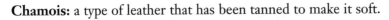

Chamois: a type of leather that has been tanned to make it soft.

Claying: the process of using a clay bar (similar to Play–Doh) to remove contaminants from the surface of paint after a vehicle is washed and dried.

Clearcoat: a protective coating over the base coating of paint that protects the color from oxidizing.

Cutting/finishing pad: used on a rotary buffer/polisher to correct surface irregularities in paint or to polish paint to a high shine.

dba: "doing business as;" refers to the name you choose for your business, even if it has your own name in it (as in Dave's Auto Detailing and Car Spa).

Demographics: the primary characteristics of your target audience, such as age, gender, ethnic background, income level, education level, and home ownership.

Detailing clay: a product used to remove surface contamination, like particles and paint overspray, from a vehicle's painted surfaces.

Dressing: the process of applying cleaning/conditioning products.

Express detailing: an appearance–care service completed within 15 minutes after vehicle washing; often includes vacuuming, cleaning/dressing of interior surfaces, and other detailing processes.

Fogger odor remover: a product used to neutralize and destroy odors, especially in carpet, velour, leather, and vinyl, as well as ventilation systems; also commonly known as "odor bombs."

Goldplating: the application of gold finish to automotive chrome and stainless steel; often used to recondition or give a new look to vehicle emblems.

Headliner: the fabric that lines a vehicle's ceiling.

Logo (or logotype): an identifying symbol used by organizations.

Loupe: a photographer's tool that detailers use to detect or examine flaws in paint.

Masking: covering up the paint, chrome, fabric, or other materials next to the area of the vehicle being worked on to prevent damage; often done with masking tape alone or with newspaper affixed with masking tape.

Overspray removal: removal of chemical contaminants like asphalt, tar, concrete, industrial fallout, and paint deposited on vehicle paint and trim.

Ozone odor remover: an air purification device that removes odors caused by smoke, mold, fungi, and bacteria.

Paint leveler: a product used to remove grit scratches without leaving swirls.

Paint thickness gauge: a device that measures the thickness of paint to determine how thick the clearcoat is.

Paintless dent repair: a technique that removes door dings and hail damage from automotive finishes.

Polish: a paint conditioner used to restore oil to automotive paint, remove fine scratches, and create high gloss; compare to "wax."

Pressure washer: a device for delivering water under high pressure; also used for applying cleaning products.

Quality–of–finish measurement instrument: a device for measuring and evaluating automotive finishes.

Rail dust: iron dust particles created by friction between train wheels and train tracks that settle on the finish of vehicles transported by rail, which then corrode and become embedded in the finish.

Random orbital polisher: a power tool used for buffing and shampooing; operates in an irregular circular pattern.

Rotary buffer/polisher: tool for correcting surface irregularities on paint and/or polishing paint to a high shine; it doesn't apply torque to the surface and operates in a random pattern.

Sand trap/oil separator: type of sewage equipment that removes pollutants from water generated by businesses like detailers before the water is discharged into the sewer system.

Swirl marks: fine scratches in a circular pattern on vehicle finishes caused by using a buffer incorrectly.

Tank sprayer: a pressurized container for delivering chemicals.

Temperature gauge: a device for checking the surface temperature of paint.

Wastewater reclamation system: equipment used to contain and capture wastewater and chemical runoff from detailing operations.

Wax: a substance used to protect a vehicle's shine; applied after polish.

Wet–dry vac: a less expensive alternative to a carpet extractor.

Index